MARTIN LUTHER

SPIRITUAL LEADERS AND THINKERS

MARY BAKER EDDY

MOHANDAS GANDHI

AYATOLLAH RUHOLLAH KHOMEINI

MARTIN LUTHER

AIMEE SEMPLE McPHERSON

THOMAS MERTON

DALAI LAMA (TENZIN GYATSO)

SPIRITUAL
LEADERS AND
THINKERS

MARTIN LUTHER

Samuel Willard Crompton

Introductory Essay by
Martin E. Marty, Professor Emeritus
University of Chicago Divinity School

CHELSEA HOUSE
PUBLISHERS
A Haights Cross Communications Company

Philadelphia

CHELSEA HOUSE PUBLISHERS

VP, NEW PRODUCT DEVELOPMENT Sally Cheney
DIRECTOR OF PRODUCTION Kim Shinners
CREATIVE MANAGER Takeshi Takahashi
MANUFACTURING MANAGER Diann Grasse

Staff for MARTIN LUTHER

EXECUTIVE EDITOR Lee Marcott
SENIOR EDITOR Tara Koellhoffer
PRODUCTION EDITOR Megan Emery
ASSISTANT PHOTO EDITOR Noelle Nardone
SERIES AND COVER DESIGNER Keith Trego
LAYOUT 21st Century Publishing and Communications, Inc.

www.chelseahouse.com

First Printing

9 8 7 6 5 4 3 2 1

Library of Congress Cataloging-in-Publication Data applied for.

ISBN 0-7910-7863-9

CONTENTS

Foreword

Why become acquainted with notable people when making efforts to understand the religions of the world?

Most of the faith communities number hundreds of millions of people. What can attention paid to one tell about more, if not most, to say nothing of *all*, their adherents? Here is why:

The people in this series are exemplars. If you permit me to take a little detour through medieval dictionaries, their role will become clear.

In medieval lexicons, the word *exemplum* regularly showed up with a peculiar definition. No one needs to know Latin to see that it relates to "example" and "exemplary." But back then, *exemplum* could mean something very special.

That "ex-" at the beginning of such words signals "taking out" or "cutting out" something or other. Think of to "excise" something, which is to snip it out. So, in the more interesting dictionaries, an *exemplum* was referred to as "a clearing in the woods," something cut out of the forests.

These religious figures are *exempla*, figurative clearings in the woods of life. These clearings and these people perform three functions:

First, they define. You can be lost in the darkness, walking under the leafy canopy, above the undergrowth, plotless in the pathless forest. Then you come to a clearing. It defines with a sharp line: there, the woods end; here, the open space begins.

Great religious figures are often stumblers in the dark woods.

We see them emerging in the bright light of the clearing, blinking, admitting that they had often been lost in the mysteries of existence, tangled up with the questions that plague us all, wandering without definition. Then they discover the clearing, and, having done so, they point our way to it. We then learn more of who we are and where we are. Then we can set our own direction.

Second, the *exemplum*, the clearing in the woods of life, makes possible a brighter vision. Great religious pioneers in every case experience illumination and then they reflect their light into the hearts and minds of others. In Buddhism, a key word is *enlightenment*. In the Bible, "the people who walked in darkness have seen a great light." They see it because their prophets or savior brought them to the sun in the clearing.

Finally, when you picture a clearing in the woods, an *exemplum*, you are likely to see it as a place of cultivation. Whether in the Black Forest of Germany, on the American frontier, or in the rain forests of Brazil, the clearing is the place where, with light and civilization, residents can cultivate, can produce culture. As an American moviegoer, my mind's eye remembers cinematic scenes of frontier days and places that pioneers hacked out of the woods. There, they removed stones, planted, built a cabin, made love and produced families, smoked their meat, hung out laundered clothes, and read books. All that can happen in clearings.

In the case of these religious figures, planting and cultivating and harvesting are tasks in which they set an example and then inspire or ask us to follow. Most of us would not have the faintest idea how to find or be found by God, to nurture the Holy Spirit, to create a philosophy of life without guidance. It is not likely that most of us would be satisfied with our search if we only consulted books of dogma or philosophy, though such may come to have their place in the clearing.

Philosopher Søren Kierkegaard properly pointed out that you cannot learn to swim by being suspended from the ceiling on a belt and reading a "How To" book on swimming. You learn because a parent or an instructor plunges you into water, supports you when necessary, teaches you breathing and motion, and then releases you to swim on your own.

Kierkegaard was not criticizing the use of books. I certainly have nothing against books. If I did, I would not be commending this series to you, as I am doing here. For guidance and courage in the spiritual quest, or—and this is by no means unimportant!—in intellectual pursuits, involving efforts to understand the paths others have taken, there seems to be no better way than to follow a fellow mortal, but a man or woman of genius, depth, and daring. We "see" them through books like these.

Exemplars come in very different styles and forms. They bring differing kinds of illumination, and then suggest or describe diverse patterns of action to those who join them. In the case of the present series, it is possible for someone to repudiate or disagree with *all* the religious leaders in this series. It is possible also to be nonreligious and antireligious and therefore to disregard the truth claims of all of them. It is more difficult, however, to ignore them. Atheists, agnostics, adherents, believers, and fanatics alike live in cultures that are different for the presence of these people. "Leaders and thinkers" they may be, but most of us do best to appraise their thought in the context of the lives they lead or have led.

If it is possible to reject them all, it is impossible to affirm everything that all of them were about. They disagree with each other, often in basic ways. Sometimes they develop their positions and ways of thinking by separating themselves from all the others. If they met each other, they would likely judge each other cruelly. Yet the lives of each and all of them make a contribution to the intellectual and spiritual quests of those who go in ways other than theirs. There are tens of thousands of religions in the world, and millions of faith communities. Every one of them has been shaped by founders and interpreters, agents of change and prophets of doom or promise. It may seem arbitrary to walk down a bookshelf and let a finger fall on one or another, almost accidentally. This series may certainly look arbitrary in this way. Why precisely the choice of these exemplars?

In some cases, it is clear that the publishers have chosen someone who has a constituency. Many of the world's 54 million Lutherans may be curious about where they got their name, who the man Martin Luther was. Others are members of a community but choose isolation: The hermit monk Thomas Merton is typical. Still others are exiled and achieve their work far from the clearing in which they grew up; here the Dalai Lama is representative. Quite a number of the selected leaders had been made unwelcome, or felt unwelcome in the clearings, in their own childhoods and youth. This reality has almost always been the case with women like Mary Baker Eddy or Aimee Semple McPherson. Some are extremely controversial: Ayatollah Ruhollah Khomeini stands out. Yet to read of this life and thought as one can in this series will be illuminating in much of the world of conflict today.

Reading of religious leaders can be a defensive act: Study the lives of certain ones among them and you can ward off spiritual—and sometimes even militant—assaults by people who follow them. Reading and learning can be a personally positive act: Most of these figures led lives that we can indeed call exemplary. Such lives can throw light on communities of people who are in no way tempted to follow them. I am not likely to be drawn to the hermit life, will not give up my allegiance to medical doctors, or be successfully nonviolent. Yet Thomas Merton reaches me and many non-Catholics in our communities; Mary Baker Eddy reminds others that there are more ways than one to approach healing; Mohandas Gandhi stings the conscience of people in cultures like ours where resorting to violence is too frequent, too easy.

Finally, reading these lives tells something about how history is made by imperfect beings. None of these subjects is a god, though some of them claimed that they had special access to the divine, or that they were like windows that provided for illumination to that which is eternal. Most of their stories began with inauspicious childhoods. Sometimes they were victimized, by parents or by leaders of religions from which they later broke.

Some of them were unpleasant and abrasive. They could be ungracious toward those who were near them and impatient with laggards. If their lives were symbolic clearings, places for light, many of them also knew clouds and shadows and the fall of night. How they met the challenges of life and led others to face them is central to the plot of all of them.

I have often used a rather unexciting concept to describe what I look for in books: *interestingness.* The authors of these books, one might say, had it easy, because the characters they treat are themselves so interesting. But the authors also had to be interesting and responsible. If, as they wrote, they would have dulled the personalities of their bright characters, that would have been a flaw as marring as if they had treated their subjects without combining fairness and criticism, affection and distance. To my eye, and I hope in yours, they take us to spiritual and intellectual clearings that are so needed in our dark times.

Martin E. Marty
The University of Chicago

1

Pope, Monk, and Salesman

I am well aware that I am of
mean condition and no consequence.

—Martin Luther to Archbishop Albert

Sometime in the early autumn of 1517, Brother Martin Luther began to hear word of the sales of indulgences. Luther was a monk, a member of the Order of the Hermits of St. Augustine in Wittenberg, Germany. The reports he heard came from parishioners and friends who had crossed the border from Saxony, of which Wittenberg was a part, into nearby Brandenberg. Both Saxony and Brandenberg were electorates, meaning that they were ruled by one of the seven electors of the Holy Roman Empire, which corresponded roughly to what is now Germany.

Brother Luther was a skillful theologian who had spent many years in the study of the Bible. He, like many other members of his monastic order, distrusted the great importance that had recently been placed upon the sale of indulgences. Since these indulgences were authorized by none other than Pope Leo X, however, friars were reluctant to say too much against them.

An indulgence was simply a piece of paper, duly authorized by the pope, which granted remission of the temporal penalty for sins. The temporal (or worldly) penalty was separated from the spiritual (or otherworldly) penalties: The Church promised nothing concerning these latter. But from where had this idea come?

As early as 1300, Pope Boniface VIII had announced the theory behind indulgences. The actions of Jesus Christ, the Apostles, and the saints who had come after them had created a "Treasury of Merits" in heaven. This spiritual "bank account" could be drawn upon by the pope to grant remission of penalty for sins. Never, though, had Pope Boniface declared that all sins could be erased, or that one could purchase one's own way out of Purgatory: One had to do it for one's relatives.

The theory had proved to be worth its weight in coins. About a million pilgrims had come to Rome during the Jubilee Year of 1300. They had visited the shrines and relics of saints, and paid for indulgences. The theory had worked in practice, and every pope from Boniface to Leo had authorized the sale of at least some indulgences. This was nothing new.

Something else had to have happened to push Brother Luther over the edge to disobedience. After all, the three greatest vows a monk took were those of poverty, chastity, and obedience—meaning obedience to all superiors, not just the pope in Rome. But something had indeed happened: Pope Leo had authorized the selling of indulgences on a massive scale, in order to pay for the building of a new St. Peter's Basilica in Rome. The pope had cut a deal to help his plans along.

The deal was as follows: Albert Hohenzollern, the twenty-seven-year-old archbishop of Brandenberg, wished to become the archbishop of Mainz as well. Since, by holding the first position, Albert was also the church administrator of Heidelberg, this meant that he would, in effect, hold three church offices at the same time. This was a crime in those days, often referred to as "clerical pluralism."

The Catholic, or Universal, Church had penalties for such behavior, but popes also had the power to grant special dispensations. Pope Leo X granted Archbishop Albert such a dispensation because of the benefit that would accrue to the Church.

Sometime early in 1517, Albert borrowed 27,000 *gulden* (the German unit of money) from the House of Fugger, which was the largest banking concern in northern Europe (the largest in southern Europe was the House of Medici). Albert paid 10,000 gulden directly to Rome, where it went at once into the general fund for the building of St. Peter's. Work on the basilica had commenced in 1507, but it was far from finished. It is unclear exactly what Archbishop Albert did with the other 17,000 gulden, but in any event, he was required to pay back the full 27,000 to the Fuggers. To help Albert pay the debt, Pope Leo authorized the sale of many indulgences in Germany, and allowed Albert and the Fuggers to split the sums collected between them. It was a truly unholy bargain.

What was different about this 1517 sale of indulgences from earlier popes' efforts? It was the sheer size and scale of the operation. Pope Leo authorized Archbishop Albert to hire men to hawk the indulgences throughout Germany, and these men used all sorts of unethical means to make sales. One of the most famous (or infamous) salesmen was the Dominican friar Johann Tetzel. One cartoon of the time showed him riding on horseback, calling out, "As soon as the coin in the coffer rings, the soul from purgatory springs!" [1]

Tetzel and other salesmen confused the issue. Rather than holding to the traditional belief and theory that indulgences were only for the remission of punishment for sins here on Earth, Tetzel persuaded people that they could buy their deceased relatives' way out of time spent in Purgatory: the place where souls went to do penance before they could enter heaven.

One might ask: Why would people believe something like this? The very question, though, shows the great difference between our age and that of Johann Tetzel, Pope Leo, and Martin Luther. Men and women of that day lived in a state of fear and dread, at least so far as their souls were concerned. The Catholic Church had long been the only major faith in Europe: Jews and Muslims were small minorities. Most Europeans believed, at least to some extent, in devils, angels, and other supernatural phenomena. They lived in a world quite different from the secular one we inhabit in the twenty-first century.

The more Luther heard about the indulgence sales, the angrier he became. Luther knew that many of the people who bought the indulgences were illiterate; they could not read the printed certificates they purchased to determine whether they were even legitimate. As the son of a copper miner and the grandson of a hardworking peasant, Luther believed it was his duty to inform people that they were being deceived. But here was the problem: How could he do it?

To accost Johann Tetzel or another indulgence salesman on the street was certainly not beneath Luther's dignity. He was a large, powerful man, with a forceful appearance. But to resort to a physical confrontation would merely provoke trouble on one street corner; it would not reach many other people. Therefore,

Luther resorted to the tool with which he was most familiar: his pen. He wrote out in longhand his Ninety-five Theses (they were printed soon afterward), which he posted on the church door at Wittenberg on October 31, 1517. They began:

> Out of love and zeal for truth and the desire to bring it to light, the following theses will be publicly discussed at Wittenberg under the chairmanship of the reverend father Martin Luther, Master of Arts and Sacred Theology and regularly appointed Lecturer on these subjects at that place. He requests that those who cannot be present to debate orally with us will do so by letter. In the name of our Lord Jesus Christ. Amen.[2]

On that same day, October 31, Luther sent a copy of the Ninety-five Theses to Archbishop Albert. Luther's cover letter indicates either that he did not know about the archbishop's part in the sale of indulgences, or that he was willing to give Albert the benefit of the doubt. Luther began in humble terms:

> Pardon me, if I, a man of no standing, should yet have the temerity to think of writing to your Sublime Excellency. The Lord Jesus is my witness that I am well aware that I am of mean condition and no consequence; and I have therefore long deferred doing what I am now making bold to do.[3]

This was a little overdone, but monks prized their humility. Luther went on to address the situation:

> Papal indulgences for building St. Peter's are being carried round under the authority of your most distinguished self. The purpose of the protest I am now making is not concerned with the substance of the message which the preachers proclaim so loudly; for I have not myself actually heard them; but I do deplore the very mistaken impressions which the common people have gained.[4]

This was Luther's gift—to speak for the common people of Germany. He came from humble origins himself, and did not seek profit or preferment. This lack of personal ambition, coupled with a burning desire to see the Scriptures read and properly interpreted, made Luther quite possibly the most dangerous man of the age.

Luther had started a religious revolution. Europe would never be quite the same again.

2

The Catholic Church From 1200 to 1513

The papacy had triumphed over conciliarism,
but it failed to reestablish its moral and
spiritual leadership over Christendom.

—Historian Thomas Boken Kotter,
A Concise History of the Catholic Church

One way to tell the story of the Catholic Church is simply to list the popes who reigned, whether in Rome or Avignon. But another, perhaps more effective, way is to describe the theological and political controversies that surrounded the Church over the centuries.

In about the year 1200, the Catholic Church was the most powerful institution to be found anywhere in Europe. Innocent III was the pope. He had great ambitions for the papacy and for himself. So powerful did he become that, in 1210, King John I of England actually admitted, in a document, that he was a vassal of Pope Innocent III, and that he held England as a fief, meaning that he had to profess continued loyalty to Rome just for the right to hold the kingdom. This moment of King John's humiliation and of Pope Innocent's glory is often seen as the absolute high point of papal power.

At the same time, there were many people who believed that the Church had become too worldly, too involved in the ways and means of kingdoms and empires. Some people believed that the Church had become a symbol of the world, rather than the beacon by which a Christian might navigate his or her way through the world. One such person was Francis Bernardone of the village of Assisi in northern Italy.

Born the son of an Italian cloth merchant, Francis experienced a playful and romantic youth. It is not certain what turned him around—perhaps it was a serious illness—but he suddenly became very pious and devout. Francis worked by himself, rebuilding old dilapidated churches. He also displayed an extraordinary talent for communicating with animals. Young men and women began to flock to him, but they discovered that to join Francis was no light matter. When he said "poverty, chastity, and obedience," he meant it.

Poverty was the vow that Francis took the most seriously. His followers were to abstain from any personal ownership. Nothing but the clothing on their backs was to be their own, and they were expected to beg for their dinner every night. Francis's instructions were quite explicit: "The Brothers must beware not to accept church buildings, or poor dwellings, or anything else built for them not in accordance with holy poverty . . . ; they should occupy these places only as strangers and pilgrims."[5]

Despite the severity of Francis's teachings, a number of young men and women joined him as unofficial disciples. News of this young man and his followers spread to Rome, where the aged Pope Innocent III was living out his last years. Tradition has it that Innocent immediately approved of the spirit behind Francis's work, and in 1209, he gave papal approval to the new order known as the Franciscans (the official name is the Friars Minor). When Francis died in 1226, his work had been accomplished. He had created the first of the three groups known as the mendicant (begging) friars.

The second group was founded by Dominic of Spain. His calling was less severe than that of Francis, and his new order was devoted to preaching rather than service. But the Dominicans, as they soon became known, were also mendicant friars, and they, too, helped improve the image of the Catholic Church. One could argue that, without the activities of Francis and Dominic, the Catholic Church might have undergone a reformation long before it actually did.

The third group of mendicants, to which Martin Luther would later belong, was the Order of the Hermits of St. Augustine. Since they were named for St. Augustine (354–430) and not for any reformer of their own period, one would imagine that the Augustinians would be more traditional and less reform-minded than either the Franciscans or the Dominicans. This proved generally to be the case, but many important leaders of the Church came from Augustinian ranks. Their order was officially founded in 1256.

The Catholic Church was strengthened and given greater dignity through the efforts of the mendicant friars. Even cynical Europeans, who were accustomed to hearing about the abuses that existed in Rome, were impressed by the sights of Franciscans, Dominicans, and Augustinians doing their work calmly and patiently in the world. They tended the sick, raised money for orphans and widows, and worked to make the world better than the way they had found it. Even as the mendicant friars accomplished their tasks, though, the papacy continued to expand its vision for universal rule.

In 1300, Pope Boniface VIII declared a Jubilee Year, in which pilgrims to Rome would receive greater credit toward indulgences than ever before. The Jubilee Year was a great success, but Pope Boniface's life and pontificate soon went in a descending spiral. In 1302, he issued *Unam Sanctam*, a papal bull that declared—if anyone had actually wondered—that the pope and the pope alone had the right to decide matters of Church doctrine (often called "dogma"). Theologians and professors could continue to discuss matters of Scripture and faith, but the Church itself spoke with one voice: that of the pope.

Boniface died in 1303, after the papal palace at Anagni, Italy, was attacked by a group of mercenary soldiers. His successor soon decided to leave Rome. He sought sanctuary from King Philip the Fair of France and moved to lovely Avignon on the banks of the Rhône River in southern France. There, the papacy remained from 1309 until 1377. This period has often been called the Babylonian Captivity of the papacy, a reference to the time when the Jews were held as prisoners in Babylon.

If the Church had been held suspect before, the removal of the popes to Avignon caused even further suspicion. After all, the papacy now seemed to be a mere tool of the kings of France. Most European Christians were greatly relieved when the papacy returned to Rome in 1377, but even then, the troubles were not over. Due to contests between men who were sponsored by the pope and others who were sponsored by the Holy Roman emperor, there was, for a time, more than one pope.

Public concern grew to the point where there was a demand for a conciliar movement, meaning that councils would be called to address the future of the Church. The papacy was dead set against this proposal, but the presence of more than one pope had led to a crisis that was impossible to deny. So, in 1414, a large council of bishops and archbishops met at Constance, Switzerland, to determine the future direction of the faith.

Hand-in-hand with the period of Babylonian Captivity had been the appearance of two important reformers: Jan Hus and John Wycliffe. The former was Bohemian (Czech) and the latter was English. Between them, these men managed to rock the foundations of papal supremacy.

Born in England in 1328, John Wycliffe was both a professor at Oxford University and, in later years, the rector of Lutterworth in Leicestershire. His political patron, John of Gaunt, protected him from the many dangers to which his unorthodox beliefs exposed him.

Both in his preaching and in his writing, John Wycliffe distinguished between the "visible Church" and the "true Church." The former was obvious: It included the pope, cardinals, bishops, and priests. The latter was more subtle: The true Church was composed of all the good Christians who had ever lived and died. According to this line of thinking, every good Christian could be viewed as both one of the faith's believers and as someone who could aspire to priesthood. It was these people who made up the true Church, in Wycliffe's view.

Wycliffe was most interested in separating what was actually written in the Scriptures from Church policies that had developed over hundreds of years. He saw nothing in the Scriptures that called for a pope or an extensive bureaucracy. Wycliffe wanted the Church to return to its early roots. He stayed in England and did not once venture to the Continent, where he might have been arrested by papal agents. Wycliffe had the good fortune to live in England, where some of the leaders and many of the common people had a natural suspicion of the Roman aspect of the Catholic Church. True, King John I had once agreed that he held his entire kingdom as a fief under Pope Innocent III, but ever since then, the English Church had kept a wary eye on its own independence. John Wycliffe died peacefully in 1384; his followers came to be known as the Lollards, and the Church branded their beliefs the "Lollard heresy."

Born in 1372, Jan Hus preached in and around the great city of Prague, in what is now Czechoslovakia. He gradually came to the idea that Holy Communion (the sharing of bread and wine at the Mass) could be distributed by worthy lay members of the congregation as well as by the priest. This was challenged fiercely by the Church's doctors of law, but Jan Hus dared them to find anything in either the Old or New Testament to prove him wrong. When they failed to do so, Hus continued the practice. His followers became known as Hussites, and the Catholic Church branded their movement the "Hussite heresy."

The Church was able to do little about Hus so long as there was more than one pope. In 1414, a great council began its meetings at Constance, Switzerland. Years would pass before the council succeeded in its work, but at the end, in 1417, there would be one pope rather than two or even three.

The council examined more than the papal dispute alone, though. At one point, Jan Hus was ordered to come to Constance to defend his views.

Hus's many followers derided the very idea. They knew what might happen to their beloved leader. But Sigismund VI, the Holy Roman emperor, gave his word that Hus would not be harmed: that he would be under the safe conduct of the imperial power. Hus, however, was a faithful son of the Church, who disagreed with a particular doctrine, and that put him in a vulnerable position. Knowing the danger, he went to Constance anyway, where he was tried, sentenced, and burned to death. The emperor's word had been worthless; the Church leaders simply said that promises made to heretics did not have to be kept.

Germans and Bohemians long remembered what happened to Jan Hus. When the Reformation came, Martin Luther and other leaders were urged not to let themselves fall into the same trap.

The Catholic Church in Rome, however, did not seem to have learned much from the long period of confusion and conflict that ended at the Council of Constance. Just a few years after the council disbanded, the pope had returned to the earlier ways of making decrees and issuing bulls without regard for conciliar opinion.

One reason for the continued arrogance of the pope and his successors was the fear of "the Turk." The Ottoman Turks had captured Constantinople in 1453 and threatened all of Eastern Europe. In such a time of crisis, the papacy became more powerful than ever, as the leading spokesperson for a Christian Europe united against the Turks. There was another factor, though, which was probably even more important in enhancing the power of the papacy. This was Renaissance humanism.

Humanism is a difficult word to define properly. It may be easier to say what it is not than what it is. Humanists did not believe that humankind was naturally depraved, or that men and women needed to spend much of their time in confession and penance. Unlike the medieval outlook, which had emphasized humanity's sinful nature, Renaissance humanism declared that human beings were glorious and remarkable, and that they should push themselves to reach their full potential.

Much good came out of this new belief. The paintings and sculptures of Donatello, Raphael, Leonardo da Vinci, and Michelangelo all belong to the period of Renaissance humanism. Beautiful works of art were commissioned and executed in Rome, Florence, Milan, and Venice. Italy became the center of the world as far as artistic output and innovation was concerned.

Given that the Catholic Church had always emphasized the sinful nature of humanity, it seems odd that the papacy would embrace Renaissance humanism. But the beauty of the artwork and the effects that such works had on the common people could not be denied. Some Catholic leaders began to declare that art was essential in an age of low literacy: People who could not read the Bible could now at least see the *Pietá*, the *David*, and *The Last Supper*, and could glean some scriptural knowledge from such visual foundations. As a result, the papacy became friendly, at least to an extent, with Renaissance humanism.

The end of the fifteenth century saw the papacy both rise to new highs and sink to new lows. Rodrigo Borgia, who became Pope Alexander VI in 1492, was a highly educated man, more comfortable with Renaissance humanism than with the Old Testament. He commissioned new works of art, played a role in determining new boundary lines, and enhanced the power of the papacy. At the same time, he fathered several illegitimate children, and then did all he could to build their careers. This shameless behavior brought criticism upon the Church. Many Christians were secretly relieved when Alexander died in 1503 and was succeeded by Julius II.

Julius did not have the sexual inclinations that had led Alexander astray, but Julius was enamored of power—power in its material form, in the shape of armies, and in the sponsorship of art. Julius was the most ambitious pope since Innocent III, in that he worked to establish control over the central part of Italy, known as the Papal States. Julius also had a great love of Renaissance art and architecture. He hired Bramante and Raphael to work on the design of the new St. Peter's Basilica, and he commissioned Michelangelo to paint the ceiling of the Sistine Chapel. These works cost a great deal of money, so, in 1507, Julius declared a Jubilee Year in order to raise funds.

Pope Julius earned the biting satire of Desiderius Erasmus of Holland, one of the prominent scholars who tried to reconcile the Church with Renaissance humanism. Erasmus likened Julius to a businessman or soldier who could not see the spiritual importance of what he was doing. Nonetheless, Julius kept a firm grip on the papacy. At his death in 1513, the ceiling of the Sistine Chapel was complete, but much work remained to be done on St. Peter's. This would be the calling of the new pope, Leo X.

Born Giovanni de Medici, the new pope was the second son of Lorenzo the Magnificent, the ruler of Florence. The Medici family was as important in Italian finance as the Fuggers were in Germany, and, in the elevation of one of their own to the papacy, the Medicis appeared to have reached the summit of their ambitions. For his part, Leo was a self-indulgent man who loved pleasure in many forms, but especially in art. He is said to have declared: "Now that God has given us the papacy, let us enjoy it."[6]

Pope Leo did not know that a German monk, who had been studying the letters of St. Paul and St. Augustine, would soon rock the foundations of the Catholic Church.

3

Young Luther
and Old Germany

Help, St. Anne,
I will become a monk.

—Martin Luther

M artin Luther was born at Eiselben, Saxony, on November 11, 1483. Saxony was one of the divisions of Germany, which itself was part of the Holy Roman Empire. Something needs to be said about what the empire was and how it had grown to the point where it was about the time of Luther's birth.

The original "Roman Empire" had fallen to the Vandals, Goths, and Lombards around the year A.D. 476. For the next three hundred years, Europe had striven to rebuild itself, and in 800, Charlemagne, king of the Franks, was crowned Holy Roman emperor by Pope Leo III in Rome. From that time on, the fortunes of the Holy Roman Empire were linked with those of the papacy.

Charlemagne's empire had not lasted long, and it was replaced in 962 by the Holy Roman Empire led by King Otto of the Germans. Therefore, the Holy Roman Empire always encompassed more than just Germany: It extended across a broad swathe of Europe.

The high point of good fortune for the Holy Roman Empire had been in the eleventh century. The emperors enjoyed great power in those days, and their opinions on religious matters had to be taken into account by the pope in Rome. But starting in the twelfth century, and then accelerating in the thirteenth and fourteenth centuries, the Holy Roman Empire began to lose its political coherence. Counts, dukes, bishops, and archbishops began to assert their independence from the emperor; they and their lands remained technically part of the empire, but they administered their realms as they saw fit. Therefore, by about 1500, the Holy Roman Empire was just a shadow of its former self. It was often impossible to determine whether a person was German, Saxon, or Austrian, and whether he owed his allegiance to the emperor or to his local lord. It was into this political confusion that Martin Luther was born.

Martin's parents were Hans and Margarethe Luther. Martin was born in Eiselben, but the family soon moved to Mansfeld, where his father worked in the copper mines. Hans Luther was an aggressive, ambitious man, who wanted to move his family out of the peasant class and into the new working class. Martin Luther would later claim that he was the son and grandson of peasants but only the latter was true; Hans Luther left the family farm in his youth to seek his fortune.

Martin Luther grew up in Mansfeld, as the favored son of a hardworking father. Hans Luther prospered in mining and, as the years went by, he increasingly desired that his son should attend good schools and make a name for himself as a lawyer or administrator. Not for young Martin the hard toil of the land or the mining pits: His father wanted better for him.

Martin Luther's own recollections of his youth became

LUTHER'S PARENTS

Luther's father, Hans, has traditionally received most of the attention in accounts of Luther's family life. Stories of the strong-willed and tight-fisted miner have been used to explain Martin Luther's willpower and the resilience he showed later in life. But what about Luther's mother?

Only in 1982 did a scholar make a convincing description of Margarethe Lindemann Luther (her portrait, along with that of her husband, was painted in 1527). She came from a moderately prosperous burgher (townspeople) family. The Lindemanns had studied at the University of Erfurt before, and some of them lived in Eiselben, the town of Martin Luther's birth. Therefore, contrary to what has usually been believed, Luther's mother and her family connections were probably more important than those of his father.

Luther's parents were naturally disappointed when he chose to become a monk. He was, to their mind, throwing away the advantages they had labored so hard to put in his path. But they reconciled with their son as the years passed, and as he became the leader of the Protestant Reformation, they were proud parents. They were especially delighted when he married in 1525.

Twin paintings executed by Lucas Cranach the Elder in 1527 show two satisfied elderly people. Both Hans and Margarethe Luther have the same lively eyes that distinguished their son, but their hands, unlike his, show a lifetime of hard work that has been rewarded with social position and economic security.

increasingly hazy as the years went by. He would often recount that the Luthers were so poor that they had to forage for wood, and that his mother had to carry the wood on her back, but he failed to mention that gathering wood in the local forest was a privilege, something to which many other poor people would have aspired.

In a similar vein, Martin Luther often made his father out to be something of a tyrant, saying that he beat the son frequently. As much as we may deplore this kind of behavior today, it was quite common in the fifteenth and sixteenth centuries, and we should not ascribe too much to it: Luther was treated about the same as most children of his time. Did he bear deeper scars than many of his fellows? Was his sensitive soul more harmed by the beatings? Quite possibly. But the fact remains that Luther grew up healthy and strong, and, aside from a tempestuous nature, he never showed signs of having been abused.

Luther went to school, first in Mansfeld, and then in nearby Erfurt. Erfurt was a leading university town in northern Germany. There, Luther imbibed many of the theological controversies that had raged for decades, if not centuries. As critics of the Scholastic movement have often pointed out, the medieval schoolmasters delighted in asking questions such as: Is it permissible to eat an egg on a meatless day, when it is possible that the chick may hatch? And so forth.

Despite these seemingly bizarre teaching tactics, we should not lose sight of the value provided by the Scholastic thinkers. Starting around the time of St. Thomas Aquinas (c. 1224–1274), the Scholastics laid out an elaborate and complex set of values that became standard throughout the European world. As such, they allowed for Germans, Austrians, French, English, and Italians to communicate with one another (their letters and correspondence were done in Latin).

The Scholastic movement held primacy until the emergence of the Nominalist movement, started by the Franciscan friar William of Occam. He is best known today for his idea that the simplest and most direct answer is usually the correct one:

hence the expression, "Occam's razor." This razor-like thinking was certainly different from that of the Scholastics, and Martin Luther doubtless heard many examples of both schools of thought. The teachers at Erfurt, however, inclined toward the Nominalist movement, and Luther therefore was more accustomed the vigorous assertion of a principle or idea than the convoluted arguments often applied by the Scholastics.

One might ask: Did either the Scholastic or the Nominalist movements truly help the cause of Christianity in Europe? The answer, if given by a layperson of the time, would probably have been that no help was needed. Europe was Christian, except for the Jews who constituted about 5 percent of the population, and Christianity was Europe's gift to the world. Very few Europeans would have confessed to being agnostics, much less atheists. Christian Europe was quite safe within its own borders, but there remained the perplexing question of whether the pope or the different religious councils should hold ultimate power within the Church.

Like most young people, Luther was more interested in his immediate surroundings than with politics, whether those of the Church or the state. He appears to have been a successful student at Mansfeld, and then an excellent one at the University of Erfurt. He received his bachelor's degree there in 1502 and his master's in 1505. Again, there is some conflicting evidence concerning his circumstances. Luther later would claim he had been so poor that he needed to "sing for his dinner," and fellow students agreed that he had a melodious voice. But many students of the time engaged in this practice as part of their curriculum: It was believed to be a good way to keep them humble. So it is not certain whether Luther was, in fact, poor, or whether he was merely keeping in step with fellow students.

Hans Luther was proud of his son's achievements. Hans attended the graduation ceremony, and for the first time in his life, he addressed his son with the respectful term of *Ihr* ("you"), rather than the more familiar *Du* ("thou"). All seemed well. The son would follow in the father's footsteps by increasing the family's wealth and social position. But, just as there were conflicts between the pope and the councils, and between the Holy Roman emperor and his nobles, so, too, there were differences between Martin and Hans Luther.

The father wanted his son to become a lawyer. The son was not at all sure what he wanted to do, but he had some ideas about becoming a monk.

A monk! Nothing could be worse for the Luther family. Not only would Martin earn no income and have no children, but he would be, according to the theory of the time, "dead to the world," and therefore, dead to his relatives, too.

It is unknown whether Luther dared to raise the subject with his father. Historians are confident, however, of the event that turned Luther decisively to the Church. This happened on July 2, 1505.

Luther received his master's degree at Erfurt in January 1505. He enrolled in the university's law school that May, before going home to Mansfeld for a few weeks. After his visit home, he rode on horseback back toward school. In a story that has been told hundreds, if not thousands, of times, Luther recounted how, on his way back to school in a storm, a bolt of lightning crashed very near him, throwing him from his horse. In great fear, Luther cried out, "Help, St. Anne, I will become a monk." [7]

Anne was the patron saint of miners. As the son of a miner, it was natural that Luther would reach out to her. He did emerge from the storm, and reached Erfurt safely. Whether he would continue in the path his father wanted was another matter.

On July 6, 1505, just four days after the thunderstorm, Frederick, the elector of Saxony, created the new University of Wittenberg. Wittenberg was a smaller town than Erfurt, but it would have a profound effect on Luther's life. Eleven days later, on July 17, Luther entered the monastery of the Hermits of St. Augustine at Wittenberg. Only after he had been allowed to remain for a trial period did Luther write to his father, saying that he had decided to become a monk. We can only imagine the response of his furious father at the time.

Luther, the miner's son and peasant's grandson, had entered a monastery. Because the decision was so momentous, it appeared likely that little would be heard from Martin Luther in the future. Like every other good son of the Church, he would remain cloistered within monastery walls, and his family would receive only an occasional letter. He was, according to the rules of the time, dead to the secular world. His thoughts, however, would eventually reach beyond the monastery walls, and he would win fame in a way quite different from anything his father might have anticipated.

4

Brother Martin

God give that is
wasn't a devil's spook.

—Hans Luther to his son Martin.

L uther was not unusual for his time. Many young men entered
monasteries. Medieval Europeans greatly admired those men
and women who gave up all they had in order to serve Christ.
There were a variety of monastic orders from which to choose:
Augustinian, Benedictine, Dominican, and Franciscan, among
others. In any case, there were thousands of young men (and
women) who did what Luther did in 1505.

The first monasteries of which we have certain knowledge
came into being after the fall of the Roman Empire in the fifth
century. As the Roman world collapsed and as civilization itself
seemed threatened, many Europeans chose to live together in
groups, where they foreswore the world and its entrapments.
They, like the first Christians in the days of the Apostles,
intended to live in mutual love, charity, and hardship.

The first of the monastic orders was the Benedictines, formed
by St. Benedict of Nursia. Other groups followed, including
the powerful Order of Cluny in the ninth century, and the
Franciscans and Dominicans early in the thirteenth. The order
that Martin Luther joined in 1505, the Hermits of St. Augustine,
had been around since the middle of the thirteenth century.

Most of what we know of Luther's monastery years comes
from letters he wrote much later. He claims that he was happy as
a monk, at least at first, and that the discipline imposed by the
monastery did not grate upon his sensibilities.

In the early spring of 1507, Luther had progressed to the point
where he was about to be ordained as a priest. He wrote to John
Braun, the vicar of Eisenach and an old friend, asking him to
attend the service (this is the earliest of Luther's letters that has
been preserved):

> My father has arranged that, with God's help, I shall be
> consecrated to the office of the priesthood on Sabbath four
> weeks [from today].
>
> The day has been fixed to suit my father. Perhaps it may be
> presuming too much on your love when I humbly beg for
> your presence also. I do not ask you to make this troublesome

journey because of any services I may have rendered you, for I know of none, but because I experienced so much of your goodness when with you lately. . . .

And lastly I would remind you that you pass our cloister and must not seek other quarters! But one of our cells must content you.

May you be preserved in Christ Jesus our Lord! In our cloister at Erfurt.

(Signed) Martin of Mansfeld[8]

On the appointed day Hans Luther rode into the monastery, bringing with him about twenty Mansfeld residents, as well as twenty gulden, which he handed over to the monastery as his gift. Hans Luther appeared willing to forgive his son's rebellion, and was ready to bask in the pleasure of seeing Martin celebrate his first Mass.

Luther, however, faltered badly during the Mass. He stammered, almost lost control, and just barely managed to stagger through the ceremony. As if this were not bad enough, father and son had words at dinner following the Mass. Luther later recalled the argument:

I started to talk with him after a childish good comportment, wanting to put him in the wrong and myself in the right, by saying, "Dear father, why did you resist so hard and become so angry because you did not want to let me be a monk, and maybe even now you do not like too much to see me here, although it is a sweet and godly life, full of peace?" But there [the father] carried on, in front of all the doctors, magisters and other gentlemen, "You scholars, have you not read in the scriptures that one should honor father and mother?" And as others started to argue with him, Hans Luder said what was as good as a curse: "'God give that it wasn't a devil's spook"—referring of course to the thunderstorm on the road to Erfurt.[9]

This was not a promising beginning to Luther's career as a priest.

Luther achieved quick promotion within the monastery. He earned a master of arts in theology in record time, and in 1508, he was transferred to the monastery at Wittenberg so his talents could be showcased more easily. Sometime in 1510, Luther and a fellow brother from the monastery went to Rome—the Eternal City. They traveled by foot over the Alps in winter, and came down into Italy, which must have seemed like paradise compared to the road they had trod.

Luther wrote no letters from Rome, and he kept no diary while he was there. Again, all we have to go on today are letters he wrote many years later about his experience. The trip seems to have been very mixed. These were exciting times in Rome. Pope Julius II had recently commissioned Michelangelo to paint the ceiling of the Sistine Chapel, and numerous public works were in progress. Luther either failed to notice these or decided they were not important enough to comment upon, since his writings about the visit center squarely on the Church, in all its variations:

> I would not trade my visit to Rome for a hundred thousand gulden, even though its shameful wickedness is so great I still cannot fully comprehend it. When I first saw Rome, I fell to the ground, lifted my hands, and said, "Hail to thee, O Holy Rome." Yes, it is a truly holy place because of the sainted martyrs and the blood which they shed there. But now it is torn to pieces. . . . No one can imagine the knavery, the horrible sinfulness and debauchery that are rampant in Rome. Unless a person sees, hears, and experiences it himself, it is impossible to convince him that such great evil exists. Hence the saying: If there is a hell, then Rome must be built on top of it, for every kind of sin flourishes there: not a mere beggarly covetousness but the utterly blind covetousness of despising God, a more horrible idolatry.[10]

Luther was most shocked by the way the Holy Sacraments were performed: "I ran through about a dozen Masses in Rome and was almost prostrated by the thought that my mother and father were still alive, because I should gladly have redeemed them from purgatory with my Masses and other excellent works and prayer."[11] Luther and his fellow monk spent about a month in the Eternal City, then returned north to Germany. This visit was crucial in forming Luther's later opinions.

Luther was progressing in his studies, and his mentor wanted him to undertake a doctorate in theology. Johannes von Staupitz, head of the monastery, urged Luther to seek a doctorate because he saw that the young man's brilliant mind would never be satisfied with commonplace knowledge. If Luther wanted to be fulfilled, he would have to aim for a very high standard.

LUTHER'S SPIRITUAL ADVISOR

Everyone needs a good teacher, mentor, and advisor. Luther had all three of these in Johannes von Staupitz.

Very little is known of von Staupitz's early life. He was about fifteen years older than Luther, and became the vicar-general of the Augustinian Order in Germany around 1500. From about 1509 on, he was Luther's father confessor and spiritual advisor at the University of Wittenberg.

Von Staupitz recognized Luther's great academic potential, and insisted that the younger man go on to earn his doctorate in theology. Just as important, von Staupitz was the first person to give Luther a vision of a beneficent, loving God. Von Staupitz, in numerous conversations, urged Luther to trust in the goodness and mercy of God, and not to rely on any type of effort or work to earn salvation. This idea, which later merged with Luther's reading of the Letters of St. Paul, became the cornerstone of Luther's faith and of the new religion that he founded (Luther would say he had *rediscovered* the original message of Christ).

Von Staupitz did not follow Luther in the creation of the Lutheran faith. Von Staupitz, in fact, eventually disavowed Luther and his writings, and remained within the Roman Catholic Church. Von Staupitz resigned his position as vicar-general in 1520 and joined a Benedictine abbey. Luther's last letter to von Staupitz, dated 1523, shows that Luther deeply regretted the loss of his former spiritual advisor.

Luther obtained his doctorate in 1512, and proceeded at once to lecture on St. Paul's letters to the Corinthians and to the Galatians. These letters are considered some of the most inspired and uplifting parts of the New Testament, but it would be a mistake to think that Luther was happy or fulfilled. He was, in fact, quite unhappy, and tending toward misery.

No historian or biographer has ever convincingly explained Luther's bouts of depression. Today we might say that he had "bipolar illness," meaning that he suffered severe mood swings, and that he may have benefited from medication. An earlier generation of psychiatrists would have made much of the fact that he had betrayed his father's dream in order to find his own, and that Luther suffered great guilt as a result. But these psychological attempts to describe Luther fail to address the core of his suffering, which was, quite simply, spiritual rather than psychological.

Only someone who lived in the late Middle Ages could truly tell us what it was like to live in a world where the promise of heaven and the threat of hell were so immediate. Europeans had little doubt that Muslims and Jews would go to hell, and they were convinced that many of their own number would also fail to win passage to heaven.

Europeans believed that Christ would come back to Earth at the end of time to judge the living and the dead, and that they would be separated into two groups: the sheep and the goats. To be a goat, in medieval thought, meant to be stubborn, mechanical, and wedded to the material world. Even the most prayerful or charitable person lived in considerable fear of damnation. Luther was not at all unusual for his time; what is unusual is that he had the great intelligence and the personal insight to wrestle with his fears.

By about 1516, Luther was on the verge of an emotional and physical breakdown. He was much in demand among his fellow monks, and his reputation as a learned man had already spread. But he was in personal despair over the state of his soul. Then, suddenly, perhaps as a result of frequently reading and rereading the Gospels, Luther came upon a series of phrases by St. Paul, one of which read: "The just [or righteous] shall live by faith" (Romans 1:17). The words had been there in the New Testament all along! Why did Luther suddenly come to them, and why had not other scholars before him made more of these words?

As Luther contemplated the passage, he interpreted it to mean: "The just shall live by faith *alone*." Luther was suddenly persuaded. People had to live by faith alone; no person's good works could earn him or her a place in heaven, much less guarantee it.

History often hinges on small things that work together in surprising ways. This was certainly the case with Luther and his departure from the Roman Catholic Church. It so happened that indulgences were being bought and sold, and that common people were being deceived into thinking they could purchase grace for their departed relatives. Luther would soon set them straight.

5

The Ninety-five Theses

As soon as the coin in the coffer rings,
the soul from Purgatory springs.

—Expression used to sell
indulgences in Germany

To the best of our knowledge, Martin Luther was simply a pious son of the Catholic Church, concerned about the corruption that he saw, but he had no ambition to found a new religious order; rather, he wanted to reform the church from within. Had the papacy allowed Luther to do so, the history of Western civilization might have been quite different. Ultimately, one could say that Luther's crisis was based on a pope, an archbishop, a salesman, and a dome—St. Peter's Basilica in Rome.

During the pontificate of Julius II, a decision had been made to build a new St. Peter's. The old one, made of wood, had been destroyed by fire, and the time had come to build and dedicate a beautiful new shrine to St. Peter. Pope Julius started the work around 1506 but he died in 1513, and the project was continued by Pope Leo X. Soon after he came to the papal throne, Leo authorized an increased number of sales of indulgences, to get the funds needed to pay for the work to be done on St. Peter's.

The pope's need for money coincided with the desire of a young aristocrat to hold three church offices at the same time. Albert of Brandenberg was only twenty-four years old when he became archbishop of Brandenberg and church administrator of Heidelberg. Not only was he too young to be an archbishop, but holding two such offices amounted to clerical pluralism, one of the oft-committed Church crimes of the late Middle Ages. Two years later, Albert was elected archbishop of the diocese of Mainz as well, and he was truly in a difficult spot, since only the pope could grant an allowance for this circumstance.

Pope Leo was willing to do this, but he required the high price of 10,000 gold ducats. Even Albert could not come up with this amount, so the papal officers in Germany arranged a special deal, under which Albert borrowed money to pay the pope, who in turn allowed Albert to raise money for the repayment of his debt through the sale of indulgences in his dioceses. All told it was a rather stunning business arrangement, notable for its intricacy as well as its cynicism.

In the spring of 1517, Archbishop Albert hired a number of men to sell indulgences. One of the most active and the most successful was Johann Tetzel, a Dominican friar. Tetzel was known for his zeal in selling and for colorful expressions like, "As soon as the coin in the coffer rings, the soul from Purgatory springs."

Sales proceeded, and in the late summer and early autumn, Martin Luther heard about what was happening from his parishioners who had crossed the border into Mainz and Brandenburg. Upset by the stories, Luther obtained a copy of the instructions

ERASMUS OF ROTTERDAM

Born in Gouda, Holland, around 1466, Desiderius Erasmus became the most revered intellectual figure of his time. Long before Luther came to prominence, Erasmus became the greatest spokesperson for the Catholic Church, and, occasionally, its gentle critic.

Orphaned by the age of thirteen, Erasmus entered a monastery to be cared for and educated, and he spent his entire life in the bosom of the Catholic Church. He was always either within a monastery or traveling between monasteries. This secluded life did not prevent him from becoming the best-known literary wit of the early sixteenth century.

In 1511, Erasmus published *The Praise of Folly*, which remains to this day one of the finest satires ever written about Western civilization. In it, Erasmus poked fun at Pope Julius II, who was obviously more concerned with architecture and glory than with the saving of souls, and at the kings and queens who thought they could buy their way into God's good graces. In 1516, Erasmus put out a Greek edition of the New Testament. By this time, he was known as "Erasmus of Christendom." Kings, popes, and other leaders corresponded with him on a regular basis.

If Erasmus had been willing to go even a little further, and to join hands with Martin Luther, the two might have been able to win millions of people over to their vision of a reformed Catholic Church. But Erasmus did not follow Luther; in fact, the two men became bitterly estranged from one another.

Luther is, beyond doubt, the most important figure of the Protestant Reformation, but much that he accomplished was actually made possible by Erasmus's earlier work. The tragic point is that these two great scholars, critics, and men of wit could not join forces.

that had been issued to Johann Tetzel and other salesmen. He found them so cynical that he decided something had to be done. Among the instructions were things like:

> Kings, queens, their sons, archbishops, and other princes of high rank . . . should pay at least twenty-four Rhenish gulden. . . .
>
> Other prelates, noblemen of lesser rank, leaders in important positions, and all other who because of steady incomes or the sale of goods from other sources have a recurring annual income equal to five hundred gulden, are to pay six like gulden.
>
> Other citizens and merchants who have a regular income of two hundred gulden, are to pay three like gulden.
>
> Other citizens and craftsmen who have their own income as well as servants, one like gulden.
>
> Others of lesser means are to pay half of one gulden.[12]

Luther was horrified. Not only was the Church now going beyond its original mandate, which had been only to absolve the temporal remission of sins, but the schedule of charges had been altered to suit condition and rank in society—so that virtually *everyone* could afford to buy an indulgence.

On the last day of October, on the eve of the feast of All Saints' Day, Luther went to the church door at Wittenberg and nailed up a few sheets of paper. They contained ninety-five statements, known ever since as the Ninety-five Theses. They began:

> In the desire and with the purpose of elucidating the truth, a disputation will be held on the underwritten propositions at Wittenberg, under the presidency of the Reverend Father Martin Luther, monk of the order of St. Augustine, Master of Arts and of Sacred Theology, and ordinary lecturer in the same at that place. He therefore asks those who cannot be present and discuss the subject with us orally to do so by letter in their absence. In the name of our Lord Jesus Christ. Amen.

1. Our Lord and Master Jesus Christ in saying "Repent ye" intended that the whole life of believers should be penitence.

2. This word cannot be understood as sacramental penance, that is, the confession and satisfaction which are performed under the ministry of priests.

3. Yet it does not mean solely inner repentance; such inner repentance is worthless unless it produces various outward mortifications of the flesh.

4. The penalty of sin remains as long as the hatred of self, that is, true inner repentance, until pour entrance into the kingdom of heaven.

5. The pope neither desires nor is able to remit any penalties except those imposed by his own authority or that of the canons.

6. The pope cannot remit any guilt, except by declaring and showing that it has been remitted by God; or, to be sure, by remitting guilt in cases reserved to his judgment. If his right to grant remission in these cases were disregarded, the guilt would certainly remain unforgiven.

7. God remits guilt to no one unless at the same time he humbles him in all things and makes him submissive to his vicar, the priest.

8. The penitential canons are imposed only on the living, and, according to the canons themselves, nothing should be imposed on the dying.

9. Therefore the Holy Spirit through the pope is kind to us insofar as the pope in his decrees always makes exception of the article of death and of necessity.

10. Those priests act ignorantly and wickedly who, in the case of the dying, reserve canonical penalties for purgatory.[13]

Luther, who went on to make eighty-five more of these then-radical statements, had cast down a gauntlet. Even so, it was meant to be done in the gentle fashion of academic dispute. His years as a monk had made Luther a true professional in the use of words, and he expected soon to have debates with a few learned churchmen. It is important to note that Luther, at this time, did not want a break with Rome: He merely wanted the Roman Catholic Church to reform itself from within.

6

Luther Stands Alone

Here I stand; I can do no other.

—Martin Luther

H ad Luther written the Ninety-five Theses a century earlier, it is quite likely that they might have caused a stir, but that the uproar would have been limited to a small geographic area. The reason the case was very different in 1517 was simple: the advent of the printing press.

Developed in Mainz, Germany, around 1450, by Johannes Gutenberg, the printing press was the greatest agent of change that had been seen in hundreds of years. In terms of its importance to Europe in the late Middle Ages, the printing press had perhaps only one or two rivals: the invention of gunpowder and new techniques for plowing fields (which really came about in the early Middle Ages). In terms of changing the lives of the ordinary person, nothing came close to equaling the impact of the printing press.

Pieces of metal type were cut so that, when they were covered with ink, they produced words on a page. That page could be created in exact duplication time and time again. This was a revolutionary technical system that suddenly allowed thousands of people to read the same material, and not to have any doubts that what they read was exactly the same as what their neighbor read—no errors would have been introduced by human beings trying to copy the same texts over and over by hand. This is the power of exact duplication.

Luther's Ninety-five Theses were printed rapidly and spread around northern Germany in just two weeks after they were first posted. It is believed that they traveled to all parts of Germany within six weeks, and that they reached most parts of Christian Europe during the winter of 1517–1518. Never before in Western history had a few pages of material circulated so rapidly and been read by so many people. Luther had written the Theses in Latin, since that was the language of educated people throughout Europe. But the Theses were rapidly translated into German, French, English, and other tongues, to give Luther's work a broader audience. Suddenly, within just a few months of his bold action, Luther had become known to most of the literate people in all of Europe.

MARTIN LUTHER

Although he was a generous man, Pope Leo X (seen here, at center) had his faults as well. Leo loved to enjoy the luxuries of his day—fine music, rich clothing, and sumptuous food—and he paid for his entertainments out of the Church's treasury, which would seem quite corrupt to most modern observers. He also authorized the sale of indulgences that Luther found objectionable enough to start a religious revolution. Despite the serious schism that was taking place in his church after 1517, Leo did his best to ignore the rapidly growing Protestant Reformation for several years, continuing to focus instead on his own pursuit of pleasure.

After Luther openly defied Pope Leo X, he knew he was in danger of being arrested or even executed by leaders of the Church and empire. Although some officials were hostile toward Luther and urged his condemnation, Elector Frederick the Wise (seen here), who governed the region of Germany from which Luther came, chose to defend his subject. He had men under his orders "abduct" Luther and bring the religious rebel to Wartburg Castle, where he could be safe from his enemies.

This is a view of the quaint castle yard at Wartburg, in Thuringia, Germany, from a photograph taken between 1890 and 1900. Luther stayed at Wartburg Castle during the months of seclusion when he was under the protection of Elector Frederick the Wise.

Not all people rose up to support Luther in his attack on the Catholic Church. In fact, many openly opposed him, acting publicly to defend the Church and its traditional practices. This anonymous engraving from Luther's time depicts the controversial reformer as being inspired by Satan.

Throughout the early years of his opposition to Catholic doctrine, Luther knew he was taking a dangerous gamble. Past reformers had faced terrible persecution at the hands of Church and government officials. In fact, some did not even survive their efforts to correct abuses within the religious community. Jan Hus, for example, was burned at the stake as a heretic for his defiance of the Catholic Church. His execution is depicted in this woodcut illustration.

Luther made perhaps his most controversial break with Catholicism when he, the former monk, married Katherine von Bora, a former nun. Katherine proved to be a loyal assistant and follower to Luther, and the couple enjoyed a long and loving marriage. These dual portraits of Martin Luther and his wife were done by Lucas Cranach the Elder.

There is little doubt that Luther enjoyed the attention. He had escaped the strict household of his father twelve years earlier and had, in many ways, exchanged it for the iron rule of the Augustinian monastery. Now, for the first time, he was acting as a free agent, and he liked the feeling it brought him. These pleasant emotions were balanced, however, by the negative attention that came his way. Luther had suddenly become a hero to many people, but quite a few others saw him as a dreadful villain. The first to take up the pen against him was the Dominican friar Johann Tetzel.

Tetzel published his "Countertheses" in January 1518. Tetzel was a good scholar, but he was no match for Luther in eloquence or passion. Tetzel defended the practice of the sale of indulgences, claiming once more that it benefited everyone concerned. It was even faster than most types of prayer, he argued, since the soul left Purgatory as soon as the price of the indulgence was paid. Tetzel did not present effective arguments, though, in favor of the theory of indulgences; he merely repeated that it was a blessing for people to be able to perform this service for their departed relatives.

By now, word of Luther's actions had reached Rome. Pope Leo and the papal officials, known as the curia, were at first inclined to dismiss Luther and his writings. What harm could one German monk possibly cause? This was the very summit of the High Renaissance in Rome. Beautiful new pieces of art were being commissioned on a regular basis. The pope and his officials bothered themselves little with Luther until the monk issued a second statement, this one much longer than the first.

"Resolutions" went even further than the Ninety-five Theses. Luther now began to attack the power of the pope to determine theological matters. Luther made a subtle distinction between matters of church dogma (law) and church theology; the latter could be argued. If one looked deep into the records of Church history, there was indeed support for Luther's stand, but he now incurred the wrath of the pope. Everyone remembered what had happened to Jan Hus.

A debate between Luther and Church representative Cardinal Cajetan was scheduled for July 1518 at Augsburg. The two men debated for hours, but were unable to make any impression on each other. Where, Luther asked, was the substance of his wrongs, his possible heresy? The cardinal answered that he had questioned the right of the pope to grant indulgences, a right that traced back to a papal bull of 1347. But what was the ground, the substance, behind that papal bull, asked Luther? He and Cajetan went round and round, with neither making much headway.

Luther left Augsburg late in October and arrived home at Wittenberg on the last day of the month. It had been precisely one year since he had tacked the Ninety-five Theses on the church door, and neither he nor the papacy seemed any closer to reaching an agreement.

Back in Wittenberg, Luther took up his pen once more. Though he had intended for the Theses to be debated strictly among Church prelates, he was now convinced that the time had come to broaden his argument. He wrote his *Address to the Christian Nobility of the German Nation Concerning the Reform of the Christian Estate* in German, and thereby made another break from the medieval past. In this remarkable pamphlet, Luther described the Roman Catholic Church as being surrounded by three walls: the assertion that spiritual power was always superior to temporal power, that the pope believed he had the right to interpret the Scriptures, and that the pope's right to call a council that was ultimately subservient to his will. By dismissing the council as a legitimate means of Church reform, Luther rejected the type of compromise that had worked so often in the past. The conciliar movement of the fourteenth and fifteenth centuries would be insufficient, he argued, to reform the Church now: It needed a thorough overhaul.[14]

The *Address* was a blatant appeal to the self-interests of the German nobles. For centuries, they had vacillated between supporting the wishes of the emperor and keeping to themselves. The result was that Germany was a fractured nation, without political coherence. Luther appealed to the German knights and lords to take power into their own hands, and to do so in a way that would build a new German nation.

The appeal to nationalism was clever. Luther knew his history, and he knew that the German lords would be pleased to find some way to limit the power of the emperor. The moment, too, was propitious, since Holy Roman Emperor Maximilian I died early in 1519. Who would be his successor?

The key to the title of Holy Roman emperor lay in the votes of the seven men known as electors. These seven men had to consider dozens of different possibilities before they cast their votes, and the time was ripe for bribery. Money begat money, as several powerful European monarchs contended for the crown.

At this time, King Henry VIII of England was not yet the overweight and tyrannical person we know from his famous portraits by Hans Holbein. He still held the good will of his subjects, and his marriage to Catherine of Aragon remained full of mutual affection. The only problem was that Catherine had had only one child, a girl (the future Queen Mary). Concerned for the future of his throne, Henry was beginning to think about how he might get rid of his wife and take one who might give him a son. But first, he had one other consideration: How might he win the election and become the Holy Roman emperor?

Henry could only hope to do so if he appeared to be a faithful and loyal son of the Church. So, for the next few years, he did his best to appear more Catholic and pious than ever before. As part of that effort, Luther's writings were banned from English soil (although some still managed to get there anyhow).

King Francis I of France also aspired to the crown of Charlemagne and Otto. Francis, in his position on the Continent, was closer to the scene than Henry, and he had a good deal of money to spend toward bribing the electors. Francis spent away, hoping for the best, but in the end, he was outmatched by Charles, king of Spain.

A grandson of Maximilian on his father's side, and a grandson of Ferdinand and Isabella on his mother's, Charles was already the most powerful man in Christian Europe. He was young, however—younger than either Henry or Francis, and they both thought to take advantage of his youth. Charles's able ministers, however, persuaded him to stake everything on the election, and he sent great sums to the electors. In the middle of 1519, Charles won the election and became Holy Roman emperor–elect. His coronation was still some time off.

A more subtle or discerning pope might have taken advantage of the situation. By concentrating on the election of the new emperor, and by ignoring Martin Luther, Pope Leo could have been seen as a statesman, and, if some thought him obtuse, well, popes had survived worse than that. But Leo went on the offensive in 1519; he issued a papal ban on Luther's writings, and demanded that Luther retract them. When a papal bull was sent to Wittenberg, Luther solemnly and publicly burned it in the town square. The moment had come for a confrontation between the pope, the emperor, and the German monk.

A new decade began on January 1, 1521. The stalemate between Luther and Pope Leo continued, but it was building to a crescendo.

Charles, king of Spain and now Holy Roman emperor–elect, arrived at Worms, Germany, in January. He spoke no German; the languages with which he was most comfortable were Flemish and French. Charles was just shy of twenty years old and he bore greater responsibilities than had been held by any one European monarch since Charlemagne (742–814). Charles was determined to see the troubles through. He sent messengers to Wittenberg, promising imperial safe conduct for Luther if he agreed to come to Worms.

Luther had his doubts about the matter. Jan Hus had once been promised safety, too. But Luther knew that the moment was too important to let pass by; he had to make a stand for his beliefs. So, in the early part of April 1521, he set out for Worms.

All accounts agree that Luther received extraordinary support from many Germans along his way. He had, through the printing of his works, already become a folk hero to many people, and they turned out to cheer loudly for him. But the news was not all good. About halfway between Wittenberg and Worms, Luther learned that the emperor had ordered all his books and pamphlets to be confiscated, in preparation for having them burned.

Luther approached Worms. The German monk was accompanied by many people who wished him well; they threw flowers in his path and called him their patron. Luther, by defying the words of Pope Leo X, had given voice to what was a great deal of discontent with the Roman Catholic Church. Luther's entrance to the council was reported by Girolamo Aleandro, the legate for Pope Leo:

> I sent out one of my men, who informed me that about a hundred horsemen . . . escorted him to the city gate; sitting in a wagon with three companions, he entered the city at ten o'clock in the forenoon, surrounded by eight men on horseback, and took up his dwelling in the neighborhood of his Saxon Elector [in a house of the Knights of St. John]. As he left the wagon, a priest threw his arms around him and touched his gown three times, and afterwards boasted of it as if he had held in his hands a relic of the greatest saint. I suppose it will soon be said of him that he performs miracles. As this Luther alighted, he looked around with his demonic eyes and said, "God will be with me." Then he entered a room where many gentlemen visited him, with ten or twelve of whom he dined; after the meal was over the world flocked to see him.[15]

The papal representative clearly detested Luther. This German monk seemed to provoke either admiration and love or fear and disgust—there was no middle ground.

On April 17, 1521, Luther entered the great council hall at Worms. As he came in, Emperor Charles is said to have muttered, "This monk will never make a heretic out of me."[16] Charles was a member of the Habsburg family, which had long treasured its connection to the Roman Catholic Church.

Although Aleandro was the papal legate, it had been arranged that the actual questioning of Luther should be done by the churchman Johann Eck. The emperor and numerous knights and nobles of northern Germany listened while Eck put his questions to the German monk:

> Martin Luther: His holy and invincible imperial majesty . . . has ordered that you be called here. . . . Wherefore, I ask you . . . : First, do you acknowledge that these books here (a bundle of his books and writings in Latin and German was shown him) now named publicly to you one by one, which are published with your name as author, are yours; do you recognize them as your works or not? Next, do you wish to retract and recall them and their contents or to cling to them henceforth and to insist on them?[17]

Luther answered the first question readily enough; he was the author. But as to the second question of whether he wished to retract what he had written, he answered in a low and timid voice that he begged for some time, twenty-four hours, in which to consider. Neither Eck nor the emperor was pleased, but they agreed to put off the matter until the following day: April 18.

Luther returned at about 4:00 P.M. the next day. This time, the shades were drawn and the council hall was dark because of thunderstorms. Candles were lit throughout the hall, and shadows crept around doorways. It was an eerie moment, but both Luther and the emperor had chosen this as the time in which to make all things clear.

The same questions were put to Luther once again. Again, he acknowledged his authorship, but he attempted to skirt around the matter of retraction. As fierce and strong as he was, Luther did not wish to be condemned by the emperor or the council; he knew what had happened to heretics of the past, such as Jan Hus, who had perished at the stake a hundred years earlier. Luther explained that his works could be divided into three groups, and that he could not easily categorize them or defend them. Eck demanded a clear answer, without "horns or teeth," so that the council might know whether Luther was a faithful son of the Church or a heretic. Luther now gathered his courage and gave the answer that has been considered the hallmark for civil and religious dissenters ever since:

> Since your majesty and your lords demand a simple answer, I shall give one without horns or teeth. Unless I am convinced by the testimony of Scripture and evident reasoning I am convinced by the Sacred Scripture I have cited—for I believe neither solely the pope nor the councils, for it is evident that they have erred often and contradict one another. My conscience is captured by the Word of God. Thus I cannot and will not revoke, since to act against one's conscience is neither safe nor honest.[18]

He added: "Here I stand, I can do no other, so Help me God. Amen."[19]

Luther left the chamber minutes later. Emperor Charles, Johann Eck, the papal legate, and the German nobles were left to consider the import of his words. What none of them seemed to realize was that Luther had just ignited a religious revolution. For the first time in more than a thousand years, a monk had openly—indeed brazenly—defied the rule of the pope.

Luther's return to the inn was recorded by Sixtus Oelhafen:

> It is now more than an hour since he returned home to his lodging where I had waited to see him. When he entered the inn he stretched his hands upward for me and others to see, and shouted with a joyful countenance. "I've come through, I've come through!" Today I had been on my way to the hall to hear him make his speech, but there was such an enormous crowd that I could not stay. Every street that he crossed was always full of people eager to see him. There is much talk and ado about him.[20]

Luther remained in Worms for several days. Emperor Charles continued to ply the German Diet, hoping to persuade the

German noblemen to condemn Luther. When he found this impossible, Charles made a dramatic and personal appeal:

> I am descended from a long line of Christian emperors of this noble German nation, and of the Most Catholic kings of Spain, the archdukes of Austria, and the dukes of Burgundy. They were all faithful to the death, to the Church of Rome, and defended the Catholic faith and the honor of God. I am resolved to follow in their steps. One single friar who goes counter to all Christianity for a thousand years must be wrong. Therefore I am resolved to stake my lands, my friends, my body, my blood, my life, and my soul. Not only I, but you of this noble German nation, would be forever disgraced if by our negligence not only heresy but the very suspicion of heresy were to endure. After having listened yesterday to the obstinate assertions of Luther, I regret that I have so long delayed in proceeding against him and his false teaching. I will have nothing more to do with him. He may have his safe-conduct for returning home, but without preaching or making any disturbances. I shall now institute proceedings against him as a notorious heretic, and herewith ask you to declare yourselves.[21]

This was a powerful speech. No one who listened doubted Charles's sincerity, or the force of his opinion. But when he claimed he would cast down everything, his body, blood, life, and soul, people may have wondered. Martin Luther had already done this; he had already put himself into this type of peril. It was clear that the emperor would not, in fact, suffer in any way for cleaving closely to the official line of the Catholic Church.

Extensive bartering went on for the next few days. At first, all seven electors of the Holy Roman Empire were willing to go along with Charles and declare Luther an outlaw. But when push came to shove, both the elector of Saxony and the elector of the Palatinate backed off: They did not sign the declaration. The German Diet was soon suspended, and Emperor Charles continued on his journey to Rome, to arrange his coronation.

Meanwhile, what became of Luther? He left Worms on April 22 without fanfare. He headed back to Wittenberg, but did not make it there. As he crossed some of the Black Hills of Thuringia—the land of his peasant ancestors—Luther was apprehended and taken off by a group of horsemen. People at first thought the abduction must be the emperor's doing, but this was quickly denied. Luther was missing for the next three months.

FREDERICK THE WISE

The Holy Roman emperor was elected by seven men, four of whom were lords and three archbishops. The seven men were known as the electors, and Frederick the Wise, duke of Saxony, was one of them.

Born about fifteen years before Luther, Frederick the Wise became known as a cagey administrator and diplomat. He played a major role in the bribery and maneuvering that led to Charles's becoming the new emperor. Then came the crisis over Martin Luther and the sale of indulgences.

Frederick was certainly torn over the matter. On the one hand, he liked Luther's stand against the emperor and central authority, since a diminished imperial presence meant more local control—and more power for him. On the other hand, Frederick had collected at Wittenberg one of the largest of all the reliquaries (shrines that hold sacred relics) seen in Christian Europe; it was said that one could release his or her relatives from thousands of years in Purgatory simply by visiting Frederick's reliquary.

Surprisingly, Frederick decided to cast his lot with Luther and the Reformation. Though he never broke openly with the emperor, Frederick kept Luther safe during the crisis time of 1520–1523. The Wittenberg reliquaries were not attacked by Luther's followers; there was a tacit agreement to respect the relics owned by Luther's patron and benefactor. Frederick the Wise died in 1525. Luther seldom acknowledged the extent of his debt to Frederick, calling him "Frederick the Unready" or "Frederick the Cautious."

7

The Lutheran Reformation

Lo! how far the glory of the church has departed!

—Martin Luther

Luther was now hidden from the sight of most Germans. Some of his letters from this period have survived. One was to his supporter Philip Melanchthon (who later went on to be the foremost theologian and writer—besides Luther himself—in the early Lutheran tradition), written on May 26, 1521:

> Do not be anxious about me, for I am very well, but my weak faith still torments me. My withdrawal from the scene of conflict is of no great moment; for, although glad to be excluded from the heavy responsibility connected with God's Word, yet for the honor of that Word we would rather burn amid fiery coals, than rot solitary and half-alive, if it were God's will.
>
> We have often talked of faith and hope, so let us try for once to put our theory into practice, seeing God has brought it all about, and not we ourselves. If I perish it will be no loss to the gospel, for you far surpass me, and as Elisha was endued with a double portion of Elijah's spirit after his ascension, so may you be enabled to follow on. . . .
>
> In the region of the birds who sing beautifully on the trees, praising God night and day, with all their might.[22]

Much of what Luther wrote in these days echoes the letters of St. Paul, who had said to the Corinthians, "Fear not," for he had learned how to live in whatever situation the Lord had seen fit to place him.

Where was this "region of the birds?" Where had Luther gone? He was in hiding at Wartburg Castle in Saxony. He had been spirited away by men in the service of Frederick the Elector—those who were supposedly his "abductors." At the castle, Luther disguised himself as Junker George (a Junker is a member of the aristocracy). This says something for Luther's adaptability. He had been a monk for nearly fifteen years, and now suddenly he had become a layman; he made a convincing Junker, but his restless spirit did not allow him to enjoy this brief period of anonymity.

One of the most revealing of Luther's letters, and one of the few that is addressed to a family member, comes from November 1521. It was written to his father, Hans Luther:

> It is almost sixteen years since I took the monk's vows without your knowledge or consent. You feared the weakness of my flesh, for I was a young fellow of 22 . . . and full of fire, and you know that the monkish life is fatal to many, and you were anxious to arrange a rich marriage for me. And for long this fear and anxiety made you deaf to those who begged you to be reconciled to me, and to give God your dearest and best. But at last you gave way, although you did not lay aside your care; for, I well remember telling you I was called through a terrible apparition from heaven, so that, when face to face with death, I made the vow, and you exclaimed, "God grant it was not an apparition of the Evil one that startled you."[23]

Luther went on to explain that God's will for him could not be thwarted:

> For He is my sole Bishop, Abbot, Prior, Lord, Father, Master! I know no other. I trust He has deprived you of your son, so that, through me, He may help the sons of many others, and prevent you rejoicing alone I know you will do no more in this matter. Although the Pope should assassinate me, and cast me into hell, he cannot raise me up again to slay me once more. . . .
>
> But, if not worthy to testify with our blood, let us cry to Him alone, and plead for mercy, so that through our life and voice we may bear witness that Jesus alone is our Lord and God—blessed to all eternity. Amen. In Whom may you be blessed, dear father—and the mother—thy Margaret, along with our whole connection—all of whom I greet in Christ Jesus. From the wilderness.
>
> [signed] Martin Luther [24]

By the beginning of 1522, Luther had put together the basic tenets of his theology. They had been many years in the making, and had benefited from his reading of St. Augustine and St. Paul, and his spirited conversations with his old mentor von Staupitz. Now Luther was ready to confront the Christian world with a new series of truths, which he believed were really rediscovered truths:

1. The Church means those who believe in Christ.

2. Though there may be hierarchies within the Church, no Christian is greater or more important than any other. All vocations are equal.

3. The Scriptures are the final authority for all Christians.

4. Man [or woman] lives by faith alone. No efforts or works, no matter how virtuous, are enough to save him. Man is saved by the grace of God's love.

Some of these Lutheran truths may seem self-evident. In the twenty-first century, the equality of persons, before the law and before God, is largely taken for granted. That was not the case in the world in which Luther grew up, however; and he, more than any other religious leader of his time, argued the case for spiritual equality.

The Lutheran principles also beg the question: Who could read the Bible of the time? A Latin edition of the New Testament had been prepared by Erasmus in 1516, but there were few Bibles in German, French, or Italian. Luther, naturally, set to work on this matter.

Luther went to Wittenberg incognito in December 1521. He went because of stories he had heard of monks giving up their vows, of monks and nuns marrying, and of the town itself on the verge of chaos. What he saw there confirmed the rumors.

Luther could have become the leader of a social revolution. Wittenberg was the testing ground for many of the social changes that would come from the Reformation, and had he embraced them all, he could have become something of a dictator. But Luther's eyes were always on the main prize—God, and humanity's relationship with God. Somewhat disturbed by what he had witnessed, Luther wrote to Frederick the Elector, asking whether he should come out of hiding.

Frederick wrote back that he could no longer protect Luther, and that if an order came from the emperor for extradition, it would have to be obeyed. Luther answered that he understood perfectly, and that Frederick had done all that was required. He, Luther, would return to Wittenberg on his own and take the consequences.

Sometime in February 1522, Luther went home. This time, his visit was in the open, and he was greeted with great rejoicing by his followers. They saw him as the one man in whom they could place perfect trust, but he did his best to warn them that only God merited such trust.

On his return Luther became the spiritual and social leader of Wittenberg. This was indeed his test case, the place in which his reforms could be put to the light of truth.

Luther proved to be more moderate than many of his disciples. Under his direction, the swift marriages between priests and nuns came to an end, and order was restored at the Wittenberg Church. Luther agreed with many of the reforms that had already taken place; most especially, he concurred that communion was a sacred rite that was not forbidden to the laity. But he moved more slowly and cautiously than those he replaced, and he generally worked with Frederick rather than in spite of him. The result was that Wittenberg became a calmer, more orderly place.

During the months of his seclusion at Wartburg Castle, Luther had been busy translating the New Testament from Latin into German. The work was arduous, but it was nearly done. Luther wrote to his friend and follower George Spalatin:

> I hope, dear Spalatin, that you have received the Gospel of St. Mark and the Epistle to the Romans with letters from good friends. The Gospel of St. Luke and the two Epistles

to the Corinthians will soon be finished. I must reply to the growling lion who calls himself King of England. The ignorance the book displays is not to be wondered at in a royal author, but the bitterness and lies are gigantic. How Satan rages! But I shall embitter him more.[25]

The "growling lion" was, of course, King Henry VIII. Still very much a faithful son of the Catholic Church at this time,

KING HENRY VIII

Some scholars sum up the great movements of the Reformation to the activities of three men: Martin Luther, King Henry VIII, and John Calvin. In this case, one can say that the Reformation was guided by a monk, a king, and a lawyer.

Born in 1491, Henry took the throne in 1509. He married the Spanish princess Catherine of Aragon, and the couple had a good relationship for many years. They failed to produce a son, however, and Henry—whose father had come to the throne through a victory in the Wars of the Roses—knew the peril that might ensue if he did not provide an heir for the kingdom. He therefore created the new Church of England in order to obtain a divorce from Catherine, after the pope refused to allow one.

Henry changed dramatically as the years went by. Early in his reign, he had been strong and handsome, but greed and gluttony caught up with him in his forties. He became very overweight and extremely demanding. Constantly hoping to get his longed-for son, he proceeded to take five wives in succession after Catherine. They were: Anne Boleyn (who was beheaded for supposedly cheating on the king), Jane Seymour (who died after childbirth, but did give Henry his only son, the future King Edward VI), Anne of Cleves (whom Henry divorced, claiming he disliked her looks), Katherine Howard (who, like Anne Boleyn, was beheaded for infidelity to the king), and Katherine Parr, who had the good luck to survive him. In his day and age, Henry was exceeded only by Tsar Ivan the Terrible (1530–1584), who had seven or eight wives: Historians do not agree on the number.

It seems that Martin Luther was more prescient than one might think when, in 1524, he wrote that he had to answer the "growling lion who calls himself King of England."

he addressed a series of disputations against Luther and his followers. King Henry's writing in *Assertio Septem Sacramentorum* (*Defense of the Seven Sacraments*) was so strongly Catholic that Pope Leo X gave the English king the honorary title of "Defender of the Faith."

Luther's translation of the New Testament came out in print in September 1522 and it immediately received the name *Septemberbibel*. The Bible caused an immediate sensation, even though it was not the first time a Bible had ever been printed in German (the first had been in 1463). Here was the word of God, as translated by the Great Reformer! The printing was done by Melchior Lotther in Wittenberg, and the text was accompanied by the illustrations of Lucas Cranach. One woodcut showed the Woman of Babylon (who represents evil and the attempt to pull the faithful away from God) with three papal crowns on her head. The meaning was obvious: The papacy had betrayed its purpose and become a thing of the world, sufficient unto itself. Thousands of Germans quickly purchased the Bible, and as they read it, their appreciation grew, both for Luther's rendition of Scripture and for the importance of German as a written language. Linguistic scholars believe that Luther's rendition was a critical moment for the development of "High German" as the equivalent of the "King's English."

Luther had moved from one triumph to the next in the fifteen months since he had been put under the ban of the empire. Recognized as the leader of a new religious movement, and in charge of events in Wittenberg, he had now published the most important piece of religious translation since the advent of the printing press.

Great changes still lay ahead. One of the most important was in his personal life. Though he had slowed down the pace of monks' leaving monasteries, and though he had urged priests and nuns not to rush into marriage, Luther was headed in that direction himself. Sometime in 1523, he began to court Katherine von Bora, and in 1524, the two married. Luther had come full circle. The obedient son had fled his father and become a monk. The obedient monk had become a contentious professor and then a religious rebel. The religious rebel had virtually started his own church, and now, in 1524, at the age of forty-three, he became a married man.

8

The Critical Year: 1524–1525

"It must be a man of strong character,"
she said rapidly, "like Dr. Martin Luther.
I'd marry him any day."

—Katherine von Bora

The year 1525 proved to be a major turning point in Luther's life. Needless to say, there had been important years before this. He had entered the monastery in 1505; he had written the Ninety-five Theses in 1517; and he had defied Emperor Charles V in 1521. But 1524–1525 proved to have several enormous consequences for Luther's life. He married; he supported the defeat of the Peasants' Rebellion; and he suffered the loss of his greatest political supporter, Frederick of Saxony.

The German Peasants' Rebellion, or the German Peasants' War, was the greatest international event of the year 1524–1525. The causes of this revolt were deep and varied, and they were not restricted to Germany alone.

The life of the average peasant or serf, who lived in the countryside, had grown extremely difficult by Luther's time. Peasants and serfs together made up about 70 percent of the total population of virtually every European nation, but their status had slipped since the time of the Black Death. The bubonic plague epidemic of 1347–1348 had killed perhaps as many as 23 million Europeans out of what was then a population of about 75 million. In the aftermath of this deadly plague, it became possible for many peasants to move off their lands and migrate into the new towns and cities that were springing up around Germany. By about 1500, the number of Germans who lived in towns and cities had grown to about 25 percent of the total population. As these new town dwellers became expert at making cloth or shaping saddles and harnesses, they acquired more wealth than their rural counterparts. People who had stayed in the countryside now had reason to envy those who had moved to the towns. At the same time, the lords and knights who dominated the countryside were determined to obtain increases in rents from their tenants, to make up for the stagnation of their wealth. All told, the average country dweller had more difficulties in 1500 than he or she had in 1300 or even 1400.

There had been a number of separate and isolated peasant revolts as early as 1513 and 1521, but the major force of the peasants' wrath emerged in the spring of 1524. The event began with a peaceful demonstration in Forcheim, in southwestern Germany. The peasants drafted a list of grievances, which has been preserved:

1. That they wish to have rights of common and chase over all water fowl, and game.

2. That they wish to give, or to be bound to give, no tithe from any produce other than the thirtieth sheaf, i.e. from corn, boats, barley, and wheat, and in addition to render such tithes to no one other than my gracious lord of Bamberg and not to the provost of the cathedral.

3. Concerning the consecration tax, whereas previously a third was to be rendered to the cathedral chapter, they intend not to pay it to my gracious lord or the chapter at all.

4. All clerical foundations and exempted properties on their lands shall be subject to taxation.

5. That the clergy should have recourse to civil judges in cases of rent and debt, and, once their suit is filed, they shall seek no proceedings or penalty in the ecclesiastical courts.[26]

These grievances were of a long-standing nature. They echoed the sentiments felt by millions of peasants throughout the Middle Ages; those peasants were now ready to fight for their rights or freedoms as they saw them.

The section concerning "rights of common and chase" referred to fishing and hunting. Lords and knights, throughout the Middle Ages, had tried to prevent their tenants from hunting and fishing. In a time and age where protein was hard to obtain, fish and deer or boar meat were highly prized. The peasants now demanded the right to hunt and fish.

A tithe was an extraction, whether it was called a tax or not. The Catholic Church demanded its tithe, usually a 10 percent share, of all goods that changed hands in medieval Germany.

The peasants' anger against the clergy showed itself in the fourth and fifth articles. All clerical properties should be subjected to taxation, and the clergy should have to appear in civil courts in matters of rent and debt.

This was a social revolution. The German peasants were demanding an end to at least half of the privileges and fees that made up the feudal system.

At almost exactly the same time that the Peasants' Rebellion began, Martin Luther stepped up his courtship of an escaped nun.

Katherine von Bora's life story was almost as confused and circuitous as that of Luther. Born in 1499, she had been given to a convent in Nimbschen, Saxony, at an early age. There, she had encountered many other girls in similar circumstances; they came from well-to-do, even aristocratic, families, who had given them away to the convent. Sometimes this was because of a lack of money; more often it was because there were too many children to raise in one household. Whatever the reason, Katherine and her fellow convent girls felt abandoned by their families, and believed they were doomed to lives of quiet desperation behind the convent walls.

The lives of nuns were not as demanding as those of monks, but the regimen placed upon these young women makes the modern heart shudder. Hours upon hours were spent in prayer, and much of the rest of the day was spent gardening, mending clothes, and—at all times—showing obedience to one's superiors. Not surprisingly, stories of Luther and the new Protestant Reformation came as welcome news to some of the convent girls. Sometime in 1523, Katherine von Bora and eleven of her fellow nuns decided to escape. They took refuge in a cart that carried containers of pickles and herring. Hidden in the large jars, the young women escaped from the convent and made their way to Wittenberg, where they were welcomed by Martin Luther.

Luther praised both the girls who had escaped and the merchant who helped them. By now, the Lutheran Reformation had come to embrace the idea of marriage. Luther had come a long way in this regard, considering he was brought up in a time when women were viewed with mistrust if not contempt. As the Reformation scholar Steven Ozment puts it:

> Luther and the first generation of Protestant clerics rejected the patristic tradition of ascetic sexuality in both their theology and their personal lives. This rejection was as great a revolution in traditional church teaching and practice as their challenge of the church's dogmas on faith, works, and the sacraments. They literally transferred the accolades Christian tradition had since antiquity heaped on the religious in monasteries and nunneries to marriage and the home.[27]

As early as 1520, Luther wrote: "For the joining together of a man and a woman is of divine law and is binding, however much it may conflict with the laws of men; the laws of men must give way before it without any hesitation."[28]

Luther slowly came to believe that marriage was the natural state of affairs and contentment for the vast majority of the human race. A small handful of people, he conceded, were better off not to marry in the first place, but their numbers were few. Most men and women would find their greatest happiness in a mate who would, with them, make the sacrifices and compromises that made for an enduring match. Now Luther had suddenly found someone he might consider for himself: Katherine von Bora.

He believed it was his responsibility to find husbands for all of the escaped convent girls, and he nearly succeeded. But Katherine von Bora rejected the man whom Luther had selected for her. A fictionalized description of Katherine's conversation with one of Luther's older friends went as follows:

> "Then you are absolutely opposed to marrying?" he queried wonderingly.
>
> She rose and moved to the door which he opened for her. "N-no . . ." she said with downcast eyes. "Not if the right one asks me."

She caught a glint of amusement in his eyes as he pursued quickly, "The right one! And who might that be?"

Kate was halfway down the winding stairway. She turned back to face him when she reached the threshold. "It must be a man of strong character," she said rapidly, "like Dr. Martin Luther. I'd marry him any day. Or at least a man I could look up to—like yourself. But Glatz! Never!" With a slam of the door she was gone, stumbling along the rough uneven footway.[29]

It is unclear how the courtship began, but Luther clearly saw something of value in this escaped nun, who was about seventeen years his junior. Portraits show that she was not a great beauty, but she possessed abundant energy, and there is obvious intelligence in her expression.

No one had expected Luther to marry. He was, after all, a forty-two-year-old bachelor, not to mention a former monk. But in 1524, he began to court Katherine von Bora. Luther married her in a private ceremony early in June, then married her again in a public ceremony later in the month.

People were incredulous. Was it not enough that Luther had defied the pope and then the emperor? Did he have to go so far as to break all his monastic vows and marry? Even Philip Melanchthon was slightly shocked at first. Luther, however, saw the marriage as a continuing statement of his hard-won freedom; he had come to view marriage and the begetting of children as a wholly natural way of life, one that most, if not all, people should engage in.

Meanwhile, the Peasants' Rebellion had become the greatest conflagration seen in many years. What had started with a list of grievances became a social revolution, which then became a full-fledged civil war.

Thomas Muntzer became the leader of the Peasants' Rebellion. By late 1524, the peasants had taken over many of the towns and cities of southern Germany, and threatened to expand even further. Their cause was assisted, to some degree, by the war that was then ongoing between Emperor Charles V and French King Francis I. Charles and Francis dueled with each other for control of northern Italy, while the peasants threatened to take over much of Germany.

Because of his uncompromising stand against Pope Leo in 1520 and against Emperor Charles in 1521, Luther was expected to side with the peasants. He had, after all, started a religious revolution that had virtually upended both the Catholic Church and the emphasis on celibacy. But Luther surprised everyone; he stood squarely with the princes and knights against the German peasants. In his *Against the Robbing and Murdering Hordes of Peasants*, Luther urged the German nobles to "bite, stab, and slay" the noxious revolutionaries.[30] Luther's actions, which seem contradictory to us, did not seem that way to him. He had

THOMAS MUNTZER

Rather little is known of his youth. He was born at Stoldberg in the Harz Mountains of western Germany. Muntzer attended schools in central Germany, and when Luther began the Reformation in 1517, Muntzer was superbly positioned to become one of its new leaders.

Unlike Luther, Muntzer believed in the complete equality of people, both in the eyes of God and before the law. Muntzer became a powerful lay preacher, calling for the peasants of Germany to rise up against the knights and lords. Muntzer did not actually start the Peasants' Rebellion of 1524–1525, but he soon became its most articulate leader. Muntzer and Luther by then had developed a complete aversion to one another; it could be said that Luther's reaction to the Peasants' Rebellion was at least partly personal.

The Peasants' Rebellion achieved its greatest success in the winter of 1524–1525. By early spring, the rebels were on the run everywhere. Muntzer and a large group were tracked down and killed late in May 1525.

Muntzer was, for Luther and other Reformation leaders, a despicable figure, but the German peasants saw him more as a vigorous and aggressive Robin Hood. Many German peasants concluded that Luther had never been a true friend to them; their real ally—Muntzer—was captured and beheaded for his deeds.

started a *religious* revolution, but it was not his place to lead a *political* one.

The eventful year of 1524–1525 closed with the death of Elector Frederick of Saxony, who had long been Luther's political patron. Luther had never been over-generous in his praise of the elector. He had likened Frederick to a tree that blows in the wind, and cannot make up its mind. But in truth, Frederick's resolute defense of Luther had kept the Lutheran Reformation alive through some of its darkest moments. Now, with Frederick dead, with the Peasants' Rebellion crushed, and with his new wife at his side, Luther was about to head into more relaxed times.

9

Our God He Is a Castle Strong: Luther's Later Years

We hope soon to be released from this assignment and come home.

—Martin Luther

A fictionalized description of the life of Katherine von Bora describes Luther and Katherine's reactions to a wedding gift:

> A representative of Prince Albert of Brandenberg stepped forward and handed her a package. Eagerly she opened it, exclaiming naively, "Oh Doctor, look at this twenty gulden! It's just what I can use for the house."
>
> He put his hand over hers and gently removed it. "No, Kate, I can't let you accept it."
>
> "Why not?"
>
> "Because Prince Albert is a man with whom I have had unpleasant contact. I have no reason to believe that he is my friend."
>
> "But that doesn't mean I can't have the money," Kate countered.
>
> "You are my wife, Kate, and everything you do reflects on me."
>
> Kate could not hide her disappointment. "Oh, Doctor," she frowned, "why turn everything down and give everything to others? Don't you realize how badly we need money to make this place livable. You have nothing! I have nothing! Still . . ." Her mouth quivered. Tears started to her eyes.[31]

Luther was eventually persuaded. The couple kept the money, and used it as the beginning of the funds required to turn the old Black House of the Order of St. Augustine into a proper home.

Luther and Katherine now began married life. Luther later admitted that theirs was not a typical love match. He had been attracted to her, he said, not by beauty or even by refinement, but through a sense of her practical nature. Here was a wife with whom he could work.

The couple proceeded to have six children: Hans, Elizabeth, Magdalene, Martin, Paul, and Margaretha. Theirs was a large and demanding household, but Katherine handled things with aplomb. She often had to entertain visitors and friends of her husband, as well as feed the six children. As the years passed, Luther became more and more devoted to his wife, once saying he would not exchange Venice and Austria for his "Katie."

Luther the author of hymns became more prominent after his marriage. He had always loved music, and recalled that as a student he had been required to "sing for his supper." Now, as a middle-aged man, he wrote numerous hymns, the best known of which is "Our God He Is a Castle Strong," often translated into English as "A Mighty Fortress Is Our God." The words, as translated by George MacDonald, are as follows:

> *Our God He is a Castle strong,*
> *A good mail-coat and weapon,*
> *The old knavish foe,*
> *He means earnest now;*
> *Force and cunningly sly His horrid policy,*
> *On earth there's nothing like him.*[32]

Meanwhile, leadership of the Reformation shifted ever so slightly away from Luther. He did not resist the change; secretly, he may have welcomed it. He had been the one and only leader for so long that it was a relief to have Philip Melanchthon take on more responsibility. Melanchthon became more prominent in 1530, when he headed the Lutheran delegation to the Diet of Worms.

Only nine years had passed since Luther defied the emperor at Worms, but Charles V was now older and more tired. He had seen the rapid spread of Lutheranism throughout the northern part of Germany, and the new faith threatened to strip away southern parts as well. Charles therefore summoned leading Lutherans to Worms in 1530, hoping to work out a compromise with them.

The Augsburg Confession of Faith, written by Melanchthon, was presented to Emperor Charles V on June 25, 1530.

The document affirmed all the new doctrines that Luther, Melanchthon, and others had sponsored over the past nine years. Most importantly, the Church was seen as the community of all believers, and men and women were justified through their faith rather than through any special merits.

Charles was as unhappy with the Lutheran movement as he had been in 1521. But the times had changed; they had, in fact, grown even more perilous. In 1529, a Turkish army led by the Sultan Suleiman I the Magnificent had come as far as the gates of the city of Vienna. Though the Turks had been turned back, Charles wanted to create a united Christian front against the threat from the East. He therefore grudgingly agreed to accept the Augsburg Confession, but only from people who had already converted to the Lutheran faith. He wanted no new converts, and in this the Lutherans tacitly agreed. It seemed as if the religious struggle might be over.

Luther received the news calmly. He had long since given up any belief he might once have had in the "trust of princes." He was now content to be the grand old man of his religious community. His fame assured, his family life prospering, he could afford to relax and allow Philip Melanchthon and others to carry the lion's share of the burden.

Luther and Melanchthon worked long and hard on their edition of the Bible, Old and New Testaments, in German. Their work was printed by Melchior Lotther in 1534. By then, some eighty editions of Luther's earlier New Testament had already been printed. If anyone wonders just how important Luther was to the Reformation, let them consider this simple fact: About one-third of all books and pamphlets sold in Germany between 1520 and 1530 were written by Luther.

Luther's great success with the written word was not echoed by all his contemporaries. William Tyndale had put out an English translation of the Bible and perished at the stake in Antwerp for his "crime." But England, which so far had been a great disappointment to Luther, was about to spawn a Reformation of its own.

King Henry VIII had demonstrated his support for Pope Leo X and the Catholic sacraments in his tract, *Defense of the Seven Sacraments,* written in 1520. Henry continued as a good son of the Catholic Church until the late 1520s. By then, Henry wanted to divorce his wife, Catherine of Aragon, because she had not borne him a son. Henry appealed to the pope, Clement VII, for a dispensation in order to divorce his wife. But Pope Clement recalled that Pope Julius II had granted Henry a dispensation back in 1509 so that he could marry Catherine in the first place (this had been because she had first been married to Henry's brother Arthur). Pope Clement therefore refused.

Henry waited a short time, but he was impatient to be rid of his queen so that he might marry Anne Boleyn, one of Catherine's ladies-in-waiting. In 1533, Henry began a complete break with the Roman Catholic Church. Although Henry still believed in most of the sacraments and the liturgy of Catholicism, he established a new English Church with himself as its head. As such, he was able to grant himself a divorce, and to send Catherine away from the court. Soon afterward, Henry married Anne Boleyn, who also failed to bear him a son; her life ended under the executioner's ax three years later.

In retrospect, 1536 seems to have been a year as decisive for religious history as 1525 had been in the personal life of Martin Luther. King Henry VIII completed his break with Roman Catholicism, creating the new English Church, and John Calvin, a young reformer, printed his *Institutes of the Christian Religion*, which became the basis for the new Calvinistic faith. Between them, Martin Luther, Henry VIII, and John Calvin had carried out a complete religious revolution.

Luther's main work was now accomplished. He relaxed, allowing Katherine to run the house and property, which expanded rapidly. Not only were there six children in the family, but Katherine brought in several of her relatives, and Luther had so many visitors that the house was usually quite full. Katherine, who had a much better head for business than her husband, wanted to acquire more land and property in order to ensure a prosperous old age. Luther was dead set against this; he viewed the acquisition of worldly goods, including land, as a sort of illness. But his wife prevailed and she acquired two houses in neighboring towns. Luther jested, saying she was a fancy rich woman.

Much of what we know of Luther's last years comes from the publication of his "Table Talk." As he, his family, and his friends sat around the big table in the kitchen of the old Black Monastery, Luther spewed out an incredible number of ideas and thoughts, some of which later were picked up and became German folk sayings. Among them were:

- The monks are the fleas on God Almighty's fur coat.

- When asked why he was so violent, Luther replied, "A twig can be cut with a bread knife, but an oak calls for an ax."

- God uses lust to impel men to marriage, ambition to office, avarice to earning, and fear to faith.

- Printing is God's latest and best work to spread the true religion throughout the world.

- I am a pillar of the pope. After I am gone he will fare worse.[33]

One of the darker aspects of Luther's later years was his attitude toward Jews. Luther, like most Christians of his day, viewed the Jews with suspicion. Why had they rejected Jesus Christ when he appeared? What stubbornness held them back from joining Christianity?

Unlike many of his contemporaries, Luther had originally held out some hope for the Jews. As late as 1523 he wrote in their defense, making statements to the effect that, were he born a Jew, he would never convert. He reminded his audience that Jesus had been a Jew, and his overall tone was much more tolerant than that of his time. But things had changed by about 1543, when he issued his attack: *On the Jews and Their Lies*.

The tract was a polemic against European Jews. They in their stubborn wrong-headedness had rejected Christ, and had also rejected the olive branch that Luther had offered them twenty years earlier. The words were some of the harshest Luther had ever used. Even his diatribes against the pope had usually contained some humor as well as invective, but Luther used only anger against the Jews. In one of the most pungent passages, Luther said, "We must exercise harsh mercy with fear and trembling, in the hope that we could save some [of the Jews] from the flames and embers. We must not avenge ourselves. They are under God's wrath—a thousand times worse than we could wish it upon them." [34]

The expression "We must not avenge ourselves" appears to hold out some hope, but Luther went on: "Firstly, that their synagogues or schools should be burned down. . . . Next, that their houses should be broken and destroyed in the same way. . . . Thirdly, that all their prayer books and Talmudists, in which such idolatrous lies, curses, and blasphemies are taught, should be taken from them." [35]

This horrific language, had it been used by the pope against the Lutherans, would have produced cries of outrage. But very few people stood up to denounce Luther; he was, after all, the grand old man of the Reformation.

Why this change of heart?

Luther had both rejected, and been rejected by, the Catholic Church in every imaginable way during the past twenty years. The art of compromise, if Luther had ever had it, had disappeared. By 1543, Luther was ready to castigate any foe that stood in his way, and he turned his fury on the Jews.

It is debatable whether Luther merely echoed what many Germans thought at the time, or whether he was a major agent responsible for shaping part of German anti-Semitism. Certainly, as the first great writer to discourse in German, he bears some responsibility.

The rabid feelings he showed in his writings did not seem to affect his personal life. Although he was the soul of wit and jocularity, however, Luther was not in good health. He seems to have married Katherine von Bora just in time; within a year of their wedding, he was plagued with all sorts of ailments. Psychologists have made much of the fact that Luther suffered from severe hemorrhoids, but they have overlooked that he also had kidney stones, chest pains, and the early signs of arthritis. None of this indicates that he was frail; rather, he worked himself to such a fevered pitch— translating the Bible and writing pamphlets—that he wore himself out. Nothing could stop his fertile brain, but his body was ailing throughout his later years.

By the early part of 1546, Luther felt himself close to the end. He agreed to go to Mansfeld, his childhood home, to mediate a dispute between two local nobles. His next-to-last letter to his wife was written on February 10, 1546:

> To the saintly, worrying Lady Katherine Luther, doctor at Zulsdorf and Wittenberg, my gracious dear wife: We thank you heartily for being so worried that you can't sleep, for since you started worrying about us, a fire broke out near my door and yesterday, no doubt due to your worry, a big stone, save for the dear angels, would have fallen and crushed us like a mouse in a trap. If you don't stop worrying, I'm afraid the earth will swallow us. Haven't you learned the Catechism, and don't you believe? pray and let God worry. "Cast your burden on the Lord." We are well except that Jonas banged his ankle. He is jealous of me and wanted to have something the matter with him too. We hope soon to be released from this assignment and come home.[36]

Luther died a week later, in the same village where he had

been raised. The great doctor, the learned leader, had come full circle.

Luther's last written words were:

> Nobody can understand Vergil in his Bucolics and Georgics unless he has first been a shepherd or a farmer for five years.
>
> Nobody understands Cicero in his letters unless he has been engaged in public affairs of some consequence for twenty years.
>
> Let nobody suppose that he has tasted the Holy Scriptures sufficiently unless he has ruled over the churches with the prophets for a hundred years. . . .
>
> We are beggars. That is true.[37]

Luther's body was brought back to Wittenberg. His funeral oration was delivered by Philip Melanchthon:

> I do not deny that the more ardent characters sometimes make mistakes, for amid the weakness of human nature no one is without fault. But we may say of such a one what the ancients said of Hercules, Cimon, and others: "rough indeed, but worthy of all praise." And in the church, if, as Paul says, he wars a good warfare, holding faith and a good conscience, he is said to be in the highest esteem by us. . . .
>
> The immortal monuments of his eloquence remain, nor has the power of his oratory ever been surpassed.
>
> The removal of such a man from our midst, a man of the most transcendent genius, skilled in learning, trained by long experience, adorned with many superb and heroic virtues, chosen of God for the reformation of the church, loving us all with a paternal affection—the removal of such a man from our midst calls for tears and lamentations. We are like orphans bereft of a distinguished and faithful father.[38]

Katherine von Bora outlived her husband by only six years. She endured much distress in those years, as the truce between Emperor Charles and the Lutheran nobles was broken. The imperial troops came as far as Wittenberg, and Charles is said to have been urged by his men to dig up Luther's bones and exhibit them as a warning as to what happened to heretics. Charles refused, saying, "I make war on the living, not on the dead." [39]

Katherine died in 1552. Her last words were, "I will stick to Christ as a burr to a top coat." [40]

10

The Man, the Nation, and the Religion

If Martin Luther walked down the street today, would anyone recognize him?

—German historian Heiko A. Oberman, *Luther: Man Between God and the Devil*

Luther was dead. The world would never be the same. Luther, the man of the Protestant Reformation, and the man of the hour, was gone. Who might take his place? Truly no one could. None of his contemporaries had the strength of mind and the virulence of pen to replace Luther.

There was another great reformer. Although he came after Luther, he did not follow him. John Calvin, born in Picardy, France, in 1509, wrote *Institutes of the Christian Religion* in 1536. He soon became the second-best-known figure of the Reformation, and after Luther's death, the movement's primary leader. Calvin followed much of Luther's thinking and theology, but Calvin went further in his belief that God was *omnipotent* ("all-powerful") and *omniscient* ("all-knowing"). Calvin preached a message of predestination, which meant that God already knew, before any man or woman was born, whether that person would go to heaven or to hell. Calvin was thus more pessimistic than Luther; he thought it quite likely that most souls were meant for damnation. But this grim doctrine did not persuade people to do whatever they pleased. Rather, Calvin urged them to live lives of moral righteousness, because the way conducted oneself on Earth *might* be a sign of whether they were to be one of God's elect or one of the damned.

In Geneva, Switzerland, Calvin instituted a rule of the elect, which became a model for Calvinistic communities everywhere. Calvin's ideas reached Scotland, where they became the basis for the Presbyterian Church, and they reached England, where they became the foundation of the faith of the Pilgrims and Puritans who crossed the Atlantic and settled in New England. To the Pilgrims and the Puritans, Martin Luther had been a remarkable man who had started the Reformation, but Calvin was the leader who had seen it through to its logical conclusion. Lutheranism did not reach North America until a little after 1700, when German refugees from the Palatinate, along the Rhine, came to Pennsylvania. The first Lutheran congregation was established in Philadelphia in 1745.

It might be said that Calvin had "stolen the thunder" from

Martin Luther. But Lutheranism remained the majority Protestant religion in Europe for a very long time. Even if this had not been the case, Luther would not have worried unduly. He had never believed that people could build anything that lasted for very long; the only thing that endured was God and God's relationship to humanity. If Luther had improved that relationship in any way, by clarifying the difference between good works and faith, then he had accomplished his mission.

How about the nation? What happened to Germany after Luther's death?

It had long been difficult to separate Germany from the Holy Roman Empire. The people were Germans and they spoke German, but their nationhood belonged to a concept dating back to about 962. No other European people carried such a burden; the Germans were expected in some way to revive the glories of Charlemagne and Otto I, and even, in some magical way, to bring about a return to the original Roman Empire. Such a burden was too great for Germany, or for any other nation.

Around the time of Luther's death, Germany was rent in two. The Catholics were still the majority faith in the southern cities and provinces, while the Lutherans formed the majority in the northern parts. Because Denmark and Sweden had become Lutheran nations as well, it was entirely possible that Germany might break asunder, and that the northern part might form some type of league with its Scandinavian neighbors to the north.

Knowing the danger of this possibility, Emperor Charles V summoned the princes and nobles of Germany to another conference, this time at Augsburg. In 1555, Charles and the nobles agreed to a basic formula: *cuius region, eius religio* ("as the ruler believes, so shall the subjects practice"). This meant that every German leader, whether he was the archbishop of Trier or the elector of Hesse, had the right to make his subjects practice the religion in which he believed. As painful as this formula sounds to us today, it was something of a step in the right direction. Germans could now choose. They could move from one part of their nation to another if their ruler's religion did not agree with their own. More to the point, most of the German leaders were wise enough to adopt the religion that was practiced by the majority of their subjects. An uneasy truce between Catholics and Lutherans was therefore put into place.

Emperor Charles abdicated his throne and resigned all his titles one year later. Charles was worn out from years of fighting both the Ottoman Turks to the East and the Lutheran heresy (as he saw it) within the Holy Roman Empire. At Ghent in Belgium, he passed on his Spanish possessions to his son Philip, and his German holdings to his brother Ferdinand. The result of this division was the separation of the Spanish Habsburgs from the Austrian Habsburgs. Although the two branches of the family would continue to work together in the future, the idea of one ruler—like Charles—who would unite the empire once again was gone.

About sixty years of uneasy peace followed. During those years, quite a few Lutherans returned to Catholicism. The reasons for this are unclear, but they may have stemmed from pressure exerted by neighbors and territorial rulers. In any case, by about 1600, the Catholic cause seemed much stronger in Europe than it had been for some time. In 1618, a series of political events led to a declaration of war between the Austrian Habsburgs and many of their Lutheran subjects in northern Germany. A terrible event had come upon Germany: the Thirty Years' War.

From 1618 until 1648, armies marched across Germany. Sometimes it was Protestants, led by men like King Gustavus II Adolphus of Sweden, who had the upper hand, and sometimes it was the armies of the Austrian Habsburgs, led by men like Albert von Wallenstein. In either case, the results were terrible for the German people. Armies in that time period consisted largely of mercenaries, who expected to receive regular pay from their leaders. If the money was not forthcoming—and this was often the case—then the mercenaries stole from the people. Cabbages, onions, and fresh greens were especially prized. One reason German peasants began to plant potatoes, which were just beginning to come from the New World, was that the potato, as a root crop, was easier to conceal.

When the Thirty Years' War ended in 1648, Germany was in a state of ruin. Perhaps 5 million people had lost their lives in this terrible conflict, more of them from starvation than from the sword. The Treaty of Westphalia brought back the tradition of limited toleration that had been established in 1555 at the Peace of Augsburg. Nothing more had been accomplished; thirty years of war had been for naught.

By 1648, the Holy Roman Empire was a thing of the past. The empire still existed in name, but there was no reality behind the pretense. German knights, lords, and bishops ran their territories as they pleased, with little or no mind to what the emperor might desire. This was a victory for local government, and many Germans thought they had achieved a better settlement than some of their neighbors. Russians, for example, now labored under the dictates of the Russian tsar, who was, at least in theory, all powerful.

The fallacy of this thinking was demonstrated when new, powerful nation-states such as France, Great Britain, and the Netherlands became the new leaders in Europe. Germany, because of its divided condition, was unable to compete with the great powers of the time. Not until 1871 did Germany become a unified nation, and even then unity was accomplished through the sword and the bullet: Chancellor Otto von Bismarck unified Germany through three wars, directed against Denmark, Austria, and France.

Bismarck created a new German Empire, distinct from the original Holy Roman Empire. Bismarck and other German leaders used Luther and his writings as part of their inspiration for a new Germany; they claimed that the great reformer had been the first of the real Germans, and that his works had laid a path for the eventual creation of a united nation. But Bismarck and his fellows were using rhetoric; they were twisting the words of Luther, making it seem as if he had been a great German nationalist, when in fact he had always wanted Germans to be pious and obedient rather than great and powerful. Pious and *obedient*. That second word brought about a great deal of trouble in the twentieth century.

Twice in the twentieth century Germany went to war. The first time Germany faced most of its European neighbors; the second time it took on much of the world. Years after the conclusion of World War II, historians and sociologists alike attempted to find the root of German obedience. Why, for instance, had the majority of Germans tamely done what the Nazi government of Adolf Hitler told them to do? Why had Germans rounded up German Jews and turned them over to the Nazis to be murdered? Of course, there were exceptions to the rule: Some Germans resisted heroically. But the majority had gone along with Hitler and the Nazi regime.

Historians and sociologists had the difficult task of recon-ciling the beauties of Germany with the horrific record of compliance with the Nazi regime. Not every scholar ruled the same way, but many came to believe that Luther's influence had played a role in bringing about tame submission to authority. Recall what he wrote to the German knights concerning the Peasants' Rebellion:

> If the peasant is in open rebellion, then he is outside the law of God, for rebellion is not simply murder, but it is like a great fire which attacks and lays waste a whole land. Thus, rebellion brings with it a land full of murders and bloodshed, makes widows and orphans, and turns everything upside down like a great disaster. Therefore, let everyone who can, smite, stab, and slay, secretly or openly, remembering that nothing can be more poisonous, hurtful, or devilish than a rebel. It is just as when one must kill a mad dog; if you don't strike him, he will strike you, and the whole land with you.[41]

Luther's defenders properly point out that it is unfair to place him and his writings in the context of the twentieth century. Still, numerous scholars remain convinced that

Luther's assertion of the rightful power of the German princes, lords, and knights was a precursor to, and may even have assisted in, the development of the horrors of the Nazi regime of 1933–1945.

Germans today are divided when it comes to Luther and his legacy. They remember him as a great reformer, the one who defied the power of the Church, but they are conscious of his mixed assets and attributes. In a way, Luther the German might be considered akin to his contemporary, King Henry VIII. If ever there was a truly English monarch, with the virtues and vices of that land, it might be said to be Henry, who, like Luther, defied the pope and created a new religion. Perhaps the last words should be left to the German historian Heiko A. Oberman, whose *Luther: Man Between God and the Devil*, is considered one of the finest biographies of Luther:

> If Martin Luther walked down the street today, would anyone recognize him? Would at least Luther scholars slow down? There are certainly enough pictures of him. Lucas Cranach, who knew Luther well and thought very highly of him, executed at least five portraits of him; three oil paintings and two copperplates have survived. This impressive series, though shaped by the vision and conception of one and the same artist, seems to depict completely different figures. The ascetic face of the serious monk has nothing in common with the vigorous, bearded Luther as Junker George except the broad forehead and the luminous eyes. There seem to be worlds between the monk and the squire, and yet there was only a year between the portraits, which date from 1520 and 1521. The eyes also give the face of 1532, immortalized by apprentices from the Cranach workshop, its individual stamp.[42]

Similar things have been written about King Henry VIII. The overweight, even grotesque, man painted by Hans Holbein the Younger bears no resemblance to the handsome and strong prince described in the letters of so many Englishmen. Perhaps Martin Luther and Henry VIII have this in common: They stand for their nation and their people in all their varieties. They are looking glasses in which viewers often find what they seek, but in which they may perhaps miss the truth.

APPENDIX

LUTHER'S NINETY-FIVE THESES

Out of love for the truth and the desire to bring it to light, the following propositions will be discussed at Wittenberg, under the presidency of the Reverend Father Martin Luther, Master of Arts and of Sacred Theology, and Lecturer in Ordinary on the same at that place. Wherefore he requests that those who are unable to be present and debate orally with us, may do so by letter.

In the Name our Lord Jesus Christ. Amen.

1. Our Lord and Master Jesus Christ, when He said Poenitentiam agite, willed that the whole life of believers should be repentance.

2. This word cannot be understood to mean sacramental penance, i.e., confession and satisfaction, which is administered by the priests.

3. Yet it means not inward repentance only; nay, there is no inward repentance which does not outwardly work divers mortifications of the flesh.

4. The penalty [of sin], therefore, continues so long as hatred of self continues; for this is the true inward repentance, and continues until our entrance into the kingdom of heaven.

5. The pope does not intend to remit, and cannot remit any penalties other than those which he has imposed either by his own authority or by that of the Canons.

6. The pope cannot remit any guilt, except by declaring that it has been remitted by God and by assenting to God's remission; though, to be sure, he may grant remission in cases reserved to his judgment. If his right to grant remission in such cases were despised, the guilt would remain entirely unforgiven.

7. God remits guilt to no one whom He does not, at the same time, humble in all things and bring into subjection to His vicar, the priest.

8. The penitential canons are imposed only on the living, and, according to them, nothing should be imposed on the dying.

9. Therefore the Holy Spirit in the pope is kind to us, because in his decrees he always makes exception of the article of death and of necessity.

10. Ignorant and wicked are the doings of those priests who, in the case of the dying, reserve canonical penances for purgatory.

11. This changing of the canonical penalty to the penalty of purgatory is quite evidently one of the tares that were sown while the bishops slept.

12. In former times the canonical penalties were imposed not after, but before absolution, as tests of true contrition.

13. The dying are freed by death from all penalties; they are already dead to canonical rules, and have a right to be released from them.

14. The imperfect health [of soul], that is to say, the imperfect love, of the dying brings with it, of necessity, great fear; and the smaller the love, the greater is the fear.

15. This fear and horror is sufficient of itself alone (to say nothing of other things) to constitute the penalty of purgatory, since it is very near to the horror of despair.

16. Hell, purgatory, and heaven seem to differ as do despair, almost-despair, and the assurance of safety.

17. With souls in purgatory it seems necessary that horror should grow less and love increase.

18. It seems unproved, either by reason or Scripture, that they are outside the state of merit, that is to say, of increasing love.

19. Again, it seems unproved that they, or at least that all of them, are certain or assured of their own blessedness, though we may be quite certain of it.

20. Therefore by "full remission of all penalties" the pope means not actually "of all," but only of those imposed by himself.

21. Therefore those preachers of indulgences are in error, who say that by the pope's indulgences a man is freed from every penalty, and saved;

22. Whereas he remits to souls in purgatory no penalty which, according to the canons, they would have had to pay in this life.

23. If it is at all possible to grant to any one the remission of all penalties whatsoever, it is certain that this remission can be granted only to the most perfect, that is, to the very fewest.

24. It must needs be, therefore, that the greater part of the people are deceived by that indiscriminate and highsounding promise of release from penalty.

25. The power which the pope has, in a general way, over purgatory, is just like the power which any bishop or curate has, in a special way, within his own diocese or parish.

26. The pope does well when he grants remission to souls [in purgatory], not by the power of the keys (which he does not possess), but by way of intercession.

27. They preach man who say that so soon as the penny jingles into the money-box, the soul flies out [of purgatory].

28. It is certain that when the penny jingles into the money-box, gain and avarice can be increased, but the result of the intercession of the Church is in the power of God alone.

29. Who knows whether all the souls in purgatory wish to be bought out of it, as in the legend of Sts. Severinus and Paschal.

30. No one is sure that his own contrition is sincere; much less that he has attained full remission.

31. Rare as is the man that is truly penitent, so rare is also the man who truly buys indulgences, i.e., such men are most rare.

32. They will be condemned eternally, together with their teachers, who believe themselves sure of their salvation because they have letters of pardon.

33. Men must be on their guard against those who say that the pope's pardons are that inestimable gift of God by which man is reconciled to Him;

34. For these "graces of pardon" concern only the penalties of sacramental satisfaction, and these are appointed by man.

35. They preach no Christian doctrine who teach that contrition is not necessary in those who intend to buy souls out of purgatory or to buy confessionalia.

36. Every truly repentant Christian has a right to full remission of penalty and guilt, even without letters of pardon.

37. Every true Christian, whether living or dead, has part in all the blessings of Christ and the Church; and this is granted him by God, even without letters of pardon.

38. Nevertheless, the remission and participation [in the blessings of the Church] which are granted by the pope are in no way to be despised, for they are, as I have said, the declaration of divine remission.

39. It is most difficult, even for the very keenest theologians, at one and the same time to commend to the people the abundance of pardons and [the need of] true contrition.

40. True contrition seeks and loves penalties, but liberal pardons only relax penalties and cause them to be hated, or at least, furnish an occasion [for hating them].

41. Apostolic pardons are to be preached with caution, lest the people may falsely think them preferable to other good works of love.

42. Christians are to be taught that the pope does not intend the buying of pardons to be compared in any way to works of mercy.

43. Christians are to be taught that he who gives to the poor or lends to the needy does a better work than buying pardons;

44. Because love grows by works of love, and man becomes better; but by pardons man does not grow better, only more free from penalty.

45. Christians are to be taught that he who sees a man in need, and passes him by, and gives [his money] for pardons, purchases not the indulgences of the pope, but the indignation of God.

46. Christians are to be taught that unless they have more than they need, they are bound to keep back what is necessary for their own families, and by no means to squander it on pardons.

47. Christians are to be taught that the buying of pardons is a matter of free will, and not of commandment.

48. Christians are to be taught that the pope, in granting pardons, needs, and therefore desires, their devout prayer for him more than the money they bring.

49. Christians are to be taught that the pope's pardons are useful, if they do not put their trust in them; but altogether harmful, if through them they lose their fear of God.

50. Christians are to be taught that if the pope knew the exactions of the pardon-preachers, he would rather that St. Peter's church should go to ashes, than that it should be built up with the skin, flesh and bones of his sheep.

51. Christians are to be taught that it would be the pope's wish, as it is his duty, to give of his own money to very many of those from whom certain hawkers of pardons cajole money, even though the church of St. Peter might have to be sold.

52. The assurance of salvation by letters of pardon is vain, even though the commissary, nay, even though the pope himself, were to stake his soul upon it.

53. They are enemies of Christ and of the pope, who bid the Word of God be altogether silent in some Churches, in order that pardons may be preached in others.

54. Injury is done the Word of God when, in the same sermon, an equal or a longer time is spent on pardons than on this Word.

55. It must be the intention of the pope that if pardons, which are a very small thing, are celebrated with one bell, with single processions and ceremonies, then the Gospel, which is the very greatest thing, should be preached with a hundred bells, a hundred processions, a hundred ceremonies.

56. The "treasures of the Church," out of which the pope. grants indulgences, are not sufficiently named or known among the people of Christ.

57. That they are not temporal treasures is certainly evident, for many of the vendors do not pour out such treasures so easily, but only gather them.

58. Nor are they the merits of Christ and the Saints, for even without the pope, these always work grace for the inner man, and the cross, death, and hell for the outward man.

59. St. Lawrence said that the treasures of the Church were the Church's poor, but he spoke according to the usage of the word in his own time.

60. Without rashness we say that the keys of the Church, given by Christ's merit, are that treasure;

61. For it is clear that for the remission of penalties and of reserved cases, the power of the pope is of itself sufficient.

62. The true treasure of the Church is the Most Holy Gospel of the glory and the grace of God.

63. But this treasure is naturally most odious, for it makes the first to be last.

64. On the other hand, the treasure of indulgences is naturally most acceptable, for it makes the last to be first.

65. Therefore the treasures of the Gospel are nets with which they formerly were wont to fish for men of riches.

66. The treasures of the indulgences are nets with which they now fish for the riches of men.

67. The indulgences which the preachers cry as the "greatest graces" are known to be truly such, in so far as they promote gain.

68. Yet they are in truth the very smallest graces compared with the grace of God and the piety of the Cross.

69. Bishops and curates are bound to admit the commissaries of apostolic pardons, with all reverence.

70. But still more are they bound to strain all their eyes and attend with all their ears, lest these men preach their own dreams instead of the commission of the pope.

71. He who speaks against the truth of apostolic pardons, let him be anathema and accursed!

72. But he who guards against the lust and license of the pardon-preachers, let him be blessed!

73. The pope justly thunders against those who, by any art, contrive the injury of the traffic in pardons.

74. But much more does he intend to thunder against those who use the pretext of pardons to contrive the injury of holy love and truth.

75. To think the papal pardons so great that they could absolve a man even if he had committed an impossible sin and violated the Mother of God—this is madness.

76. We say, on the contrary, that the papal pardons are not able to remove the very least of venial sins, so far as its guilt is concerned.

77. It is said that even St. Peter, if he were now Pope, could not bestow greater graces; this is blasphemy against St. Peter and against the pope.

78. We say, on the contrary, that even the present pope, and any pope at all, has greater graces at his disposal; to wit, the Gospel, powers, gifts of healing, etc., as it is written in I. Corinthians xii.

79. To say that the cross, emblazoned with the papal arms, which is set up [by the preachers of indulgences], is of equal worth with the Cross of Christ, is blasphemy.

80. The bishops, curates and theologians who allow such talk to be spread among the people, will have an account to render.

81. This unbridled preaching of pardons makes it no easy matter, even for learned men, to rescue the reverence due to the pope from slander, or even from the shrewd questionings of the laity.

82. To wit:—"Why does not the pope empty purgatory, for the sake of holy love and of the dire need of the souls that are there, if he redeems an infinite number of souls for the sake of miserable money with which to build a Church? The former reasons would be most just; the latter is most trivial."

83. Again:—"Why are mortuary and anniversary masses for the dead continued, and why does he not return or permit the withdrawal of the endowments founded on their behalf, since it is wrong to pray for the redeemed?"

84. Again:—"What is this new piety of God and the pope, that for money they allow a man who is impious and their enemy to buy out of purgatory the pious soul of a friend of God, and do not rather, because of that pious and beloved soul's own need, free it for pure love's sake?"

85. Again:—"Why are the penitential canons long since in actual fact and through disuse abrogated and dead, now satisfied by the granting of indulgences, as though they were still alive and in force?"

86. Again:—"Why does not the pope, whose wealth is to-day greater than the riches of the richest, build just this one church of St. Peter with his own money, rather than with the money of poor believers?"

87. Again:—"What is it that the pope remits, and what participation does he grant to those who, by perfect contrition, have a right to full remission and participation?"

88. Again:—"What greater blessing could come to the Church than if the pope were to do a hundred times a day what he now does once, and bestow on every believer these remissions and participations?"

89. "Since the pope, by his pardons, seeks the salvation of souls rather than money, why does he suspend the indulgences and pardons granted heretofore, since these have equal efficacy?"

90. To repress these arguments and scruples of the laity by force alone, and not to resolve them by giving reasons, is to expose the Church and the pope to the ridicule of their enemies, and to make Christians unhappy.

91. If, therefore, pardons were preached according to the spirit and mind of the pope, all these doubts would be readily resolved; nay, they would not exist.

92. Away, then, with all those prophets who say to the people of Christ, "Peace, peace," and there is no peace!

93. Blessed be all those prophets who say to the people of Christ, "Cross, cross," and there is no cross!

94. Christians are to be exhorted that they be diligent in following Christ, their Head, through penalties, deaths, and hell;

95. And thus be confident of entering into heaven rather through many tribulations, than through the assurance of peace.

APPENDIX

A MIGHTY FORTRESS IS OUR GOD
(Hymn written by Luther)

1.   A mighty Fortress is our God,
        A trusty Shield and Weapon;
        He helps us free from every need
        That hath us now o'ertaken.
        The old evil Foe
        Now means deadly woe;
        Deep guile and great might
        Are his dread arms in fight;
        On Earth is not his equal.

2.   With might of ours can naught be done,
        Soon were our loss effected;
        But for us fights the Valiant One,
        Whom God Himself elected.
        Ask ye, Who is this?
        Jesus Christ it is.
        Of Sabaoth Lord,
        And there's none other God;
        He holds the field forever.

3.   Though devils all the world should fill,
        All eager to devour us.
        We tremble not, we fear no ill,
        They shall not overpower us.
        This world's prince may still
        Scowl fierce as he will,
        He can harm us none,
        He's judged; the deed is done;
        One little word can fell him.

4. The Word they still shall let remain
   nor any thanks have for it;
   He's by our side upon the plain
   With His good gifts and Spirit.
   And take they our life,
   Goods, fame, child and wife,
   Let these all be gone,
   They yet have nothing won;
   The Kingdom our remaineth.

APPENDIX

CONCERNING CHRISTIAN LIBERTY
Letter of Martin Luther to Pope Leo X

Among those monstrous evils of this age with which I have now for three years been waging war, I am sometimes compelled to look to you and to call you to mind, most blessed father Leo. In truth, since you alone are everywhere considered as being the cause of my engaging in war, I cannot at any time fail to remember you; and although I have been compelled by the causeless raging of your impious flatterers against me to appeal from your seat to a future council—fearless of the futile decrees of your predecessors Pius and Julius, who in their foolish tyranny prohibited such an action—yet I have never been so alienated in feeling from your Blessedness as not to have sought with all my might, in diligent prayer and crying to God, all the best gifts for you and for your see. But those who have hitherto endeavoured to terrify me with the majesty of your name and authority, I have begun quite to despise and triumph over. One thing I see remaining which I cannot despise, and this has been the reason of my writing anew to your Blessedness: namely, that I find that blame is cast on me, and that it is imputed to me as a great offence, that in my rashness I am judged to have spared not even your person.

Now, to confess the truth openly, I am conscious that, whenever I have had to mention your person, I have said nothing of you but what was honourable and good. If I had done otherwise, I could by no means have approved my own conduct, but should have supported with all my power the judgment of those men concerning me, nor would anything have pleased me better, than to recant such rashness and impiety. I have called you Daniel in Babylon; and every reader thoroughly knows with what distinguished zeal I defended your conspicuous innocence against Silvester, who tried to stain it. Indeed, the published opinion of so many great men and the repute of your blameless life are too widely famed and too much reverenced throughout the world to be assailable by any man, of however great name, or by any arts. I am not so foolish as to attack one whom everybody praises; nay, it has been and always will be my desire not to attack even those whom public repute disgraces. I am not delighted at the faults of any man, since I am very conscious myself of the great beam in my own eye, nor can I be the first to cast a stone at the adulteress.

I have indeed inveighed sharply against impious doctrines, and I have not been slack to censure my adversaries on account, not of their bad morals, but of their impiety. And for this I am so far from being sorry that I have brought my mind to despise the judgments of men and to persevere in this vehement zeal, according to the example of Christ, who, in His zeal, calls His adversaries a generation of vipers, blind, hypocrites, and children of the devil. Paul, too, charges the sorcerer with being a child of the devil, full of all subtlety and all malice; and defames certain persons as evil workers, dogs, and deceivers. In the opinion of those delicate-eared persons, nothing could be more bitter or intemperate than Paul's language. What can be more bitter than the words of the prophets? The ears of our generation have been made so delicate by the senseless multitude of flatterers that, as soon as we perceive that anything of ours is not approved of, we cry out that we are being bitterly assailed; and when we can repel the truth by no other pretence, we escape by attributing bitterness, impatience, intemperance, to our adversaries. What would be the use of salt if it were not pungent, or of the edge of the sword if it did not slay? Accursed is the man who does the work of the Lord deceitfully.

Wherefore, most excellent Leo, I beseech you to accept my vindication, made in this letter, and to persuade yourself that I have never thought any evil concerning your person; further, that I am one who desires that eternal blessing may fall to your lot, and that I have no dispute with any man concerning morals, but only concerning the word of truth. In all other things I will yield to any one, but I neither can nor will forsake and deny the word. He who thinks otherwise of me, or has taken in my words in another sense, does not think rightly, and has not taken in the truth.

Your see, however, which is called the Court of Rome, and which neither you nor any man can deny to be more corrupt than any Babylon or Sodom, and quite, as I believe, of a lost, desperate, and hopeless impiety, this I have verily abominated, and have felt indignant that the people of Christ should be cheated under your name and the pretext of the Church of Rome; and so I have resisted, and will resist, as long as the spirit of faith shall live in me. Not that I am striving after impossibilities, or hoping that by my labours alone, against the furious opposition of so many flatterers, any good can be done in that most disordered Babylon; but that I feel myself a debtor to my brethren, and am bound to take thought for them, that fewer of them may be ruined, or that their ruin may be less complete, by the plagues of Rome. For many years now, nothing else has overflowed from Rome into the world—as you are not ignorant—than the laying waste of goods, of bodies, and of souls, and the worst examples of all the worst things. These things are clearer than the light to all men; and the Church of Rome, formerly the most holy of all Churches, has become the most lawless den of thieves, the most shameless of all brothels, the very kingdom of sin, death, and hell; so that not even antichrist, if he were to come, could devise any addition to its wickedness.

Meanwhile you, Leo, are sitting like a lamb , like Daniel in the midst of lions, and, with Ezekiel, you dwell among scorpions. What opposition can you alone make to these monstrous evils? Take to yourself three or four of the most learned and best of the cardinals. What are these among so many? You would all perish by poison before you could undertake to decide on a remedy. It is all over with the Court of Rome; the wrath of God has come upon her to the uttermost. She hates councils; she dreads to be reformed; she cannot restrain the madness of her impiety; she fills up the sentence passed on her mother, of whom it is said, "We would have healed Babylon, but she is not healed; let us forsake her." It had been your duty and that of your cardinals to apply a remedy to these evils, but this gout laughs at the physician's hand, and the chariot does not obey the reins. Under the influence of these feelings, I have always grieved that you, most excellent Leo, who were worthy of a better age, have been made pontiff in this. For the Roman Court is not worthy of you and those like you, but of Satan himself, who in truth is more the ruler in that Babylon than you are.

Oh, would that, having laid aside that glory which your most aban- doned enemies declare to be yours, you were living rather in the office of a private priest or on your paternal inheritance! In that glory none are worthy to glory, except the race of Iscariot, the children of perdition. For what happens in your court, Leo, except that, the more wicked and execrable any man is, the more prosperously he can use your name and authority for the ruin of the property and souls of men, for the multi- plication of crimes, for the oppression of faith and truth and of the whole Church of God? Oh, Leo! in reality most unfortunate, and sitting on a most perilous throne, I tell you the truth, because I wish you well; for if

Bernard felt compassion for Eugenius III, formerly abbot of St. Anastasius his Anastasius at a time when the Roman see, though even then most corrupt, was as yet ruling with better hope than now, why should not we lament, to whom so much further corruption and ruin has been added in three hundred years?

Is it not true that there is nothing under the vast heavens more corrupt, more pestilential, more hateful, than the Court of Rome? She incomparably surpasses the impiety of the Turks, so that in very truth she, who was formerly the gate of heaven, is now a sort of open mouth of hell, and such a mouth as, under the urgent wrath of God, cannot be blocked up; one course alone being left to us wretched men: to call back and save some few, if we can, from that Roman gulf.

Behold, Leo, my father, with what purpose and on what principle it is that I have stormed against that seat of pestilence. I am so far from having felt any rage against your person that I even hoped to gain favour with you and to aid you in your welfare by striking actively and vigorously at that your prison, nay, your hell. For whatever the efforts of all minds can contrive against the confusion of that impious Court will be advantageous to you and to your welfare, and to many others with you. Those who do harm to her are doing your office; those who in every way abhor her are glorifying Christ; in short, those are Christians who are not Romans.

But, to say yet more, even this never entered my heart: to inveigh against the Court of Rome or to dispute at all about her. For, seeing all remedies for her health to be desperate, I looked on her with contempt, and, giving her a bill of divorcement, said to her, "He that is unjust, let him be unjust still; and he that is filthy, let him be filthy still," giving myself up to the peaceful and quiet study of sacred literature, that by this I might be of use to the brethren living about me.

While I was making some advance in these studies, Satan opened his eyes and goaded on his servant John Eccius, that notorious adversary of Christ, by the unchecked lust for fame, to drag me unexpectedly into the arena, trying to catch me in one little word concerning the primacy of the Church of Rome, which had fallen from me in passing. That boastful Thraso, foaming and gnashing his teeth, proclaimed that he would dare all things for the glory of God and for the honour of the holy apostolic seat; and, being puffed up respecting your power, which he was about to misuse, he looked forward with all certainty to victory; seeking to promote, not so much the primacy of Peter, as his own pre-eminence among the theologians of this age; for he thought it would contribute in no slight degree to this, if he were to lead Luther in triumph. The result having proved unfortunate for the sophist, an incredible rage torments him; for he feels that whatever discredit to Rome has arisen through me has been caused by the fault of himself alone.

Suffer me, I pray you, most excellent Leo, both to plead my own cause, and to accuse your true enemies. I believe it is known to you in what way Cardinal Cajetan, your imprudent and unfortunate, nay unfaithful, legate, acted towards me. When, on account of my reverence for your name, I had placed myself and all that was mine in his hands, he did not so act as to establish peace, which he could easily have established by one little word, since I at that time promised to be silent and to make an end of my case, if he would command my adversaries to do the same. But that man of pride, not content with this agreement, began to justify my adversaries, to give them free licence, and to order me to recant, a thing which was certainly not in his commission. Thus indeed, when the case was in the best position, it came through his vexatious tyranny into a much worse one. Therefore whatever has followed upon this is the fault not of Luther, but entirely of Cajetan, since he did not suffer me to be silent and remain quiet, which at that time I was entreating for with all my might. What more was it my duty to do?

Next came Charles Miltitz, also a nuncio from your Blessedness. He, though he went up and down with much and varied exertion, and omitted nothing which could tend to restore the position of the cause thrown into confusion by the rashness and pride of Cajetan, had difficulty, even with the help of that very illustrious prince the Elector Frederick, in at last bringing about more than one familiar conference with me. In these I again yielded to your great name, and was prepared to keep silence, and to accept as my judge either the Archbishop of Treves, or the Bishop of Naumburg; and thus it was done and concluded. While this was being done with good hope of success, lo! that other and greater enemy of yours, Eccius, rushed in with his Leipsic disputation, which he had undertaken against Carlstadt, and, having taken up a new question concerning the primacy of the Pope, turned his arms unexpectedly against me, and completely overthrew the plan for peace. Meanwhile Charles Miltitz was waiting, disputations were held, judges were being chosen, but no decision was arrived at. And no wonder! for by the falsehoods, pretences, and arts of Eccius the whole business was brought into such thorough disorder, confusion, and festering soreness, that, whichever way the sentence might lean, a greater conflagration was sure to arise; for he was seeking, not after truth, but after his own credit. In this case too I omitted nothing which it was right that I should do.

I confess that on this occasion no small part of the corruptions of Rome came to light; but, if there was any offence in this, it was the fault of Eccius, who, in taking on him a burden beyond his strength, and in furiously aiming at credit for himself, unveiled to the whole world the disgrace of Rome.

Here is that enemy of yours, Leo, or rather of your Court; by his example alone we may learn that an enemy is not more baneful than a flatterer. For what did he bring about by his flattery, except evils which no king could have brought about? At this day the name of the Court of Rome stinks in the nostrils of the world, the papal authority is growing weak, and its notorious ignorance is evil spoken of. We should hear none of these things, if Eccius had not disturbed the plans of Miltitz and myself for peace. He feels this clearly enough himself in the indignation he shows, too late and in vain, against the publication of my books. He ought to have reflected on this at the time when he was all mad for renown, and was seeking in your cause nothing but his own objects, and that with the greatest peril to you. The foolish man hoped that, from fear of your name, I should yield and keep silence; for I do not think he presumed on his talents and learning. Now, when he sees that I am very confident and speak aloud, he repents too late of his rashness, and sees— if indeed he does see it—that there is One in heaven who resists the proud, and humbles the presumptuous.

Since then we were bringing about by this disputation nothing but the greater confusion of the cause of Rome, Charles Miltitz for the third time addressed the Fathers of the Order, assembled in chapter, and sought their advice for the settlement of the case, as being now in a most troubled and perilous state. Since, by the favour of God, there was no hope of proceeding against me by force, some of the more noted of their number were sent to me, and begged me at least to show respect to your person and to vindicate in a humble letter both your innocence and my own. They said that the affair was not as yet in a position of extreme hopelessness, if Leo X., in his inborn kindliness, would put his hand to it. On this I, who have always offered and wished for peace, in order that I might devote myself to calmer and more useful pursuits, and who for this very purpose have acted with so much spirit and vehemence, in order to put down by the strength and impetuosity of my words, as well as of my feelings, men whom I saw to be very far from equal to myself—I, I say, not only gladly yielded, but even accepted it with joy and gratitude, as the greatest kindness and benefit, if you should think it right to satisfy my hopes.

Thus I come, most blessed Father, and in all abasement beseech you to put to your hand, if it is possible, and impose a curb to those flatterers who are enemies of peace, while they pretend peace. But there is no reason, most blessed Father, why any one should assume that I am to utter a recantation, unless he prefers to involve the case in still greater confusion. Moreover, I cannot bear with laws for the interpretation of the word of God, since the word of God, which teaches liberty in all other things, ought not to be bound. Saving these two things, there is nothing which I am not able, and most heartily willing, to do or to suffer. I hate contention; I will challenge no one; in return I wish not to be challenged; but, being challenged, I will not be dumb in the cause of Christ my Master. For your Blessedness will be able by one short and easy word to call these controversies before you and suppress them, and to impose silence and peace on both sides—a word which I have ever longed to hear.

Therefore, Leo, my Father, beware of listening to those sirens who make you out to be not simply a man, but partly a god, so that you can command and require whatever you will. It will not happen so, nor will you prevail. You are the servant of servants, and more than any other man, in a most pitiable and perilous position. Let not those men deceive you who pretend that you are lord of the world; who will not allow any one to be a Christian without your authority; who babble of your having power over heaven, hell, and purgatory. These men are your enemies and are seeking your soul to destroy it, as Isaiah say, "My people, they that call thee blessed are themselves deceiving thee." They are in error who raise you above councils and the universal Church; they are in error who attribute to you alone the right of interpreting Scripture. All these men are seeking to set up their own impieties in the Church under your name, and alas! Satan has gained much through them in the time of your predecessors.

In brief, trust not in any who exalt you, but in those who humiliate you. For this is the judgment of God: "He hath cast down the mighty from their seat, and hath exalted the humble." See how unlike Christ was to His successors, though all will have it that they are His vicars. I fear that in truth very many of them have been in too serious a sense His vicars, for a vicar represents a prince who is absent. Now if a pontiff rules while Christ is absent and does not dwell in his heart, what else is he but a vicar of Christ? And then what is that Church but a multitude without Christ? What indeed is such a vicar but antichrist and an idol? How much more rightly did the Apostles speak, who call themselves servants of a present Christ, not the vicars of an absent one!

Perhaps I am shamelessly bold in seeming to teach so great a head, by whom all men ought to be taught, and from whom, as those plagues of yours boast, the thrones of judges receive their sentence; but I imitate St. Bernard in his book concerning *Considerations* addressed to Eugenius, a book which ought to be known by heart by every pontiff. I do this, not from any desire to teach, but as a duty, from that simple and faithful solicitude which teaches us to be anxious for all that is safe for our neighbours, and does not allow considerations of worthiness or unworthiness to be entertained, being intent only on the dangers or advantage of others. For since I know that your Blessedness is driven and tossed by the waves at Rome, so that the depths of the sea press on you with infinite perils, and that you are labouring under such a condition of misery that you need even the least help from any the least brother, I do not seem to myself to be acting unsuitably if I forget your majesty till I shall have fulfilled the office of charity. I will not flatter in so serious and perilous a matter; and if in this you do not see that I am your friend and most thoroughly your subject, there is One to see and judge.

In fine, that I may not approach you empty-handed, blessed Father, I bring with me this little treatise, published under your name, as a good omen of the establishment of peace and of good hope. By this you may perceive in what pursuits I should prefer and be able to occupy myself to more profit, if I were allowed, or had been hitherto allowed, by your impious flatterers. It is a small matter, if you look to its exterior, but, unless I mistake, it is a summary of the Christian life put together in small compass, if you apprehend its meaning. I, in my poverty, have no other present to make you, nor do you need anything else than to be enriched by a spiritual gift. I commend myself to your Paternity and Blessedness, whom may the Lord Jesus preserve for ever. Amen.

Wittenberg, 6th September, 1520.

MARTIN LUTHER'S DEFINITION OF FAITH: AN EXCERPT FROM "AN INTRODUCTION TO ST. PAUL'S LETTER TO THE ROMANS," LUTHER'S GERMAN BIBLE OF 1522

Faith is not what some people think it is. Their human dream is a delusion. Because they observe that faith is not followed by good works or a better life, they fall into error, even though they speak and hear much about faith. "Faith is not enough," they say, "You must do good works, you must be pious to be saved." They think that, when you hear the gospel, you start working, creating by your own strength a thankful heart which says, "I believe." That is what they think true faith is. But, because this is a human idea, a dream, the heart never learns anything from it, so it does nothing and reform doesn't come from this 'faith,' either.

Instead, faith is God's work in us, that changes us and gives new birth from God (John 1:13). It kills the Old Adam and makes us completely different people. It changes our hearts, our spirits, our thoughts and all our powers. It brings the Holy Spirit with it. Yes, it is a living, creative, active and powerful thing, this faith. Faith cannot help doing good works constantly. It doesn't stop to ask if good works ought to be done, but before anyone asks, it already has done them and continues to do them without ceasing. Anyone who does not do good works in this manner is an unbeliever. He stumbles around and looks for faith and good works, even though he does not know what faith or good works are. Yet he gossips and chatters about faith and good works with many words.

Faith is a living, bold trust in God's grace, so certain of God's favor that it would risk death a thousand times trusting in it. Such confidence and knowledge of God's grace makes you happy, joyful and bold in your relationship to God and all creatures. The Holy Spirit makes this happen through faith. Because of it, you freely, willingly and joyfully do good to everyone, serve everyone, suffer all kinds of things, love and praise the God who has shown you such grace. Thus, it is just as impossible to separate faith and works as it is to separate heat and light from fire! Therefore, watch out for your own false ideas and guard against good-for-nothing gossips, who think they're smart enough to define faith and works, but really are the greatest of fools. Ask God to work faith in you, or you will remain forever without faith, no matter what you wish, say or can do.

1214 King John of England acknowledges he is a vassal of Pope Innocent III

1222 Dominic of Spain forms a new order, the Dominicans

1226 Sanction is given to Francis of Assisi for his new order: the Franciscans

1256 Sanction is given to another mendicant order: the Augustinians

1300 Pope Boniface VIII declares a Jubilee Year; the concept of indulgences is added to Catholic theology

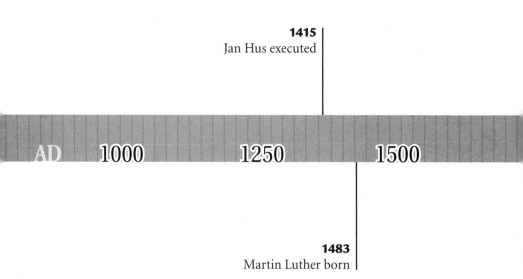

1415
Jan Hus executed

AD   1000   1250   1500

1483
Martin Luther born

1302	Boniface VIII issues *Unam Sanctum*, a papal bull
1310–1370	The popes reside at Avignon in southern France
1415	Jan Hus is burned at the stake for his heretical beliefs
1483	Martin Luther is born at Eiselben in central Germany
1501	Luther enters the University of Erfurt
1502	Elector Frederick the Wise creates the new University at Wittenberg; his collection of relics is founded there as well
1503	Pope Julius II is elected and enthroned in Rome

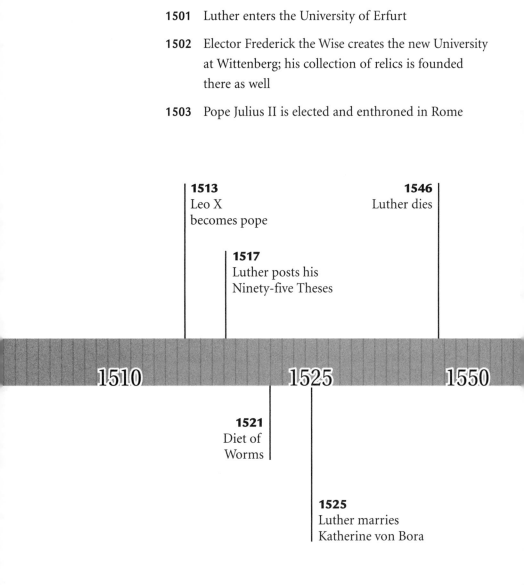

1513
Leo X
becomes pope

1546
Luther dies

1517
Luther posts his
Ninety-five Theses

1510   **1525**   **1550**

1521
Diet of
Worms

1525
Luther marries
Katherine von Bora

CHRONOLOGY

1504 Michelangelo's *David* is unveiled in Florence, Italy

1505 Luther earns his master's degree at Erfurt; makes a vow to become a monk and joins the Order of the Hermits of St. Augustine at Erfurt

1507 Pope Julius II announces plans for the building of a new St. Peter's Basilica in Rome

1509 Luther comes under the spiritual guidance of Johannes von Staupitz

1509–1510 Luther and a fellow monk travel to Rome

1512 Luther earns his doctorate in theology

1513 Michelangelo finishes the painting of the Sistine Chapel in Rome; Julius II dies and is succeeded by Pope Leo X

1516 Erasmus of Rotterdam publishes his Greek edition of the New Testament

1517 Johann Tetzel sells indulgences in Brandenberg; Luther writes his Ninety-five Theses

1518 Luther engages in academic dispute with Cardinal Cajetan

1519 Luther's writings are banned by Pope Leo X; Charles Habsburg, already king of Spain, is elected Holy Roman emperor

1520 Luther is given three months to recant his beliefs

1521 Luther goes to the Diet at Worms, where he defies Emperor Charles V; Luther goes into hiding at the Wartburg Castle

1522 Luther returns to Wittenberg; his German edition of the New Testament is printed

1523   Luther writes a tract in defense of the Jews

1524   The Peasants' Rebellion begins in southwest Germany; Luther condemns it

1525   The Peasants' Rebellion is put down amid much bloodshed; Luther marries Katherine von Bora; Luther makes a final break with Erasmus; Frederick the Wise dies

1526   Luther's first child is born

1527–1529   Luther writes the words and music for "A Mighty Fortress Is Our God"

1530   The Augsburg Confession; Luther's father dies

1543   Luther writes a vicious anti-Semitic tract

1546   Luther dies

1552   Katherine von Bora Luther dies

1555   The Peace of Augsburg establishes a fragile truce between Catholics and Lutherans in Germany

GLOSSARY

Anglican—A member of the Church of England created by King Henry VIII

Augsburg—In Swabia, Bavaria, central Germany, on the Lech River

Bohemia—Part of the Holy Roman Empire; it corresponded roughly to what is now Czechoslovakia

bull—An edict or law; when handed down by the pope, it is called a papal bull

Calvinist—A follower of the French theologian John Calvin

Constance (also Konstaz)—City on the Rhine River in southwest Germany

dispensation—An exception to a religious rule; the pope can give dispensations in special circumstances; one was given to King Henry VIII, so that he might marry his brother's widow

dogma—That part of the doctrine of any church that adherents must accept on faith

Eiselben—Town in eastern Germany at the foot of the Harz Mountains; birthplace of Martin Luther

Eisenach—Near the northern foothills of the Thuringian Forest; Luther's mother and her relatives were established burghers of this town

elector—One of the seven men who chose the new Holy Roman emperor when needed

Erfurt—City on the Gera River in central Germany

Habsburgs—The family that dominated Austria and southern Germany for centuries; a member of the family was usually elected Holy Roman emperor

Harz—Mountains in northern Germany, between the Elbe and Leine rivers

Holy Communion—The central part of the Roman Catholic Mass; the bread and wine served are believed to become the body and blood of Jesus Christ

Holy Roman emperor—Leader of a vast European territory; elected by the seven electors

Holy Roman Empire—Encompassed all of what is now Germany, and parts of what are today Austria and Switzerland

Hussite—A follower of the Czech reformer Jan Hus

indulgence—Issued by the pope, a document granting remission of the temporal punishment for sins

Lollard—A follower of the English reformer John Wycliffe

Lutheran—Today, a member of a major faith; in Luther's day, it referred to a follower of his theology

Mansfeld—The childhood home of Martin Luther

papacy—The office of the pope, the supreme leader of the Roman Catholic Church

Protestant—Someone who left the Catholic Church; the word's original meaning was "one who protests"

spiritual—In Roman Catholic theology, distinct from the temporal

temporal—Having to do with time, or the things of this world

Thuringia—A region of east-central Germany named for the Thuringian Mountains; Luther's father earned a living as a miner there

transubstantiation—The term for the miracle that takes place during the Roman Catholic Mass, in which the bread and wine literally become the body and blood of Jesus Christ. See *Holy Communion*.

Wartburg—A castle overlooking Eisenach

Wittenberg—Town in central Germany on the Elbe River; place where Luther spent most of his adult life

Worms—City on the left bank of the Rhine River in southwest Germany; seat of the Diet, or medieval German assembly

NOTES

CHAPTER 1:
Pope, Monk, and Salesman

1 Roland Bainton, *Here I Stand: A Life of Martin Luther*. New York: Abingdon Press, 1950, p. 87.
2 Oskar Thulin, ed., *A Life of Luther Told in Pictures and Narrative*, trans. Martin O. Dietrich. Philadelphia: Fortress Press, 1966, p. 30.
3 Bertram Lee Woolf, ed., *Reformation Writings of Martin Luther*. London: Lutterworth Press, 1952, p. 47.
4 Ibid., pp. 47–48.

CHAPTER 2:
The Catholic Church From 1200 to 1513

5 Heiko A. Oberman, *Luther: Man Between God and the Devil*, trans. Eileen Walliser-Schwarzbart. Garden City, NY: Doubleday, 1992; first German edition, 1982, p. 57.
6 Available online at *Bartleby.com*, *http://www.bartleby.com/67/609.html*.

CHAPTER 3:
Young Luther and Old Germany

7 Richard Marius, *Martin Luther: The Christian Between God and Death*. Cambridge: The Belknap Press, 1999, p. 43.

CHAPTER 4:
Brother Martin

8 Margaret A. Currie, ed., *The Letters of Martin Luther*. London: Macmillan, 1908, pp. 1–2.
9 Erik H. Erikson, *Young Man Luther: A Study in Psychoanalysis and History*. New York: W.W. Norton & Company, 1958, pp. 144–145.
10 Oskar Thulin, ed., *A Life of Luther Told in Pictures and Narrative*, trans. Martin O. Dietrich. Philadelphia: Fortress Press, 1966, pp. 20–21.
11 Ibid., p. 21.

CHAPTER 5:
The Ninety-five Theses

12 Oskar Thulin, ed., *A Life of Luther Told in Pictures and Narrative*, trans. Martin O. Dietrich. Philadelphia: Fortress Press, 1966, p. 29.
13 Timothy F. Lull, ed., *Martin Luther's Basic Theological Writings*. Minneapolis: Fortress Press, 1989.

CHAPTER 6:
Luther Stands Alone

14 Harry Emerson Fosdick, ed., *Great Voices of the Reformation: An Anthology*. New York: Random House, 1952, pp. 96–117.
15 Oskar Thulin, ed., *A Life of Luther Told in Pictures and Narrative*, trans. Martin O. Dietrich. Philadelphia: Fortress Press, 1966, pp. 61–62.
16 Available online at *http://www.vop.com/previous_broadcasts/1999/oct/99436.htm20*.
17 Thulin, pp. 62–63.
18 Roland Bainton, *Here I Stand: A Life of Martin Luther*. New York: Abingdon Press, 1950, p. 185.
19 Available online at *Bartleby.com*, *http://www.bartleby.com/66/25/37025.html*.
20 Thulin, p. 66.
21 Roland Bainton, *Here I Stand: A Life of Martin Luther*. New York: Abingdon Press, 1950, p. 186.

CHAPTER 7:
The Lutheran Reformation

22 Margaret A. Currie, ed., *The Letters of Martin Luther*. London: Macmillan, 1908, pp. 75–77.
23 Ibid., pp. 87–89.
24 Ibid.
25 Ibid., p. 107.

CHAPTER 8:
The Critical Year, 1524–1525

26 Tom Scott and Bob Scribner, eds. and trans., *The German Peasants' War: A History in Documents*. London: Humanities Press International, 1991, p. 81.

27 Heiko A. Oberman, *Luther: Man Between God and the Devil*, trans. Eileen Walliser-Schwarzbart. Garden City, NY: Doubleday, 1992; first German edition, 1982, p. 153.

28 Steven Ozment, *Protestants: The Birth of a Revolution*. New York: Doubleday, 1992, p. 153.

29 Clara Seuel Schreiber, *Katherine, Wife of Luther*. Philadelphia: Muhlenberg Press, 1954, p. 31.

30 Ibid., pp. 45–46.

CHAPTER 9:
Our God He Is a Castle Strong: Luther's Later Years

31 Clara Seuel Schreiber, *Katherine, Wife of Luther*. Philadelphia: Muhlenberg Press, 1954, pp. 45–46.

32 Ulrich Leupold, ed., *Luther's Works: Liturgy and Hymns*. Philadelphia: Fortress Press, 1965, vol. 53, pp. 283–285.

33 Roland Bainton, *Here I Stand: A Life of Martin Luther*. New York: Abingdon Press, 1950, p. 295.

34 Heiko A. Oberman, *Luther: Man Between God and the Devil*, trans. Eileen Walliser-Schwarzbart. Garden City, NY: Doubleday, 1992; first German edition, 1982, p. 290.

35 Ibid.

36 Roland Bainton, *Women of the Reformation in Germany and Italy*. Minneapolis: Augsburg Publishing House, 1971, p. 40.

37 Justus Jonas, Michael Coelius, et al., *The Last Days of Luther*, ed. and trans. Martin Ebon. Garden City, NY: Doubleday & Company, 1970, p. 12.

38 Harry Emerson Fosdick, ed., *Great Voices of the Reformation: An Anthology*. New York: Random House, 1952, pp. 133–135.

39 Available online at *http://www.bible.org/docs/history/schaff/vol7/schaf121.htm*.

40 Bainton, p. 42.

CHAPTER 10:
The Man, the Nation, and the Religion

41 Roland Bainton, *Here I Stand: A Life of Martin Luther*. New York: Abingdon Press, 1950, p. 280.

42 Heiko A. Oberman, *Luther: Man Between God and the Devil*, trans. Eileen Walliser-Schwarzbart. Garden City, NY: Doubleday, 1992; first German edition, 1982, p. 325.

BIBLIOGRAPHY

Bainton, Roland. *Here I Stand: A Life of Martin Luther.* Abingdon
Press, 1950.

———. *Women of the Reformation in Germany and Italy.* Augsburg
Publishing House, 1971.

Bokenkotter, Thomas. *A Concise History of the Catholic Church.*
Doubleday, 1977.

Carroll, James. *Constantine's Sword: The Church and the Jews:
A History.* Houghton Mifflin, 2001.

Carter, John, and Percy H. Muir, eds. *Printing and the Mind of Man.*
Karl Pressler, 1983.

Currie, Margaret A., ed. *The Letters of Martin Luther.* Macmillan,
1908.

Jonas, Justus, Michael Coelius, et al. *The Last Days of Luther,* ed.
and trans. Martin Ebon. Doubleday & Company, 1970.

Erikson, Erik H. *Young Man Luther: A Study in Psychoanalysis and
History.* W.W. Norton & Company, 1958.

Green, V.H.H. *Luther and the Reformation.* Capricorn Books, 1964.

Leupold, Ulrich S., ed. *Luther's Works,* vol. 53, *Liturgy and Hymns.*
Fortress Press, 1965.

Oberman, Heiko A. *Luther: Man Between God and the Devil,* trans.
Eileen Walliser-Schwarzbart. Doubleday, 1992.

Ozment, Steven. *Protestants: The Birth of a Revolution.* Doubleday,
1992.

Schreiber, Clara Seuel. *Katherine: Wife of Luther.* Muhlenberg Press,
1954.

Scott, Tom, and Bob Scribner, eds. and trans. *The German Peasants'
War: A History in Documents.* Humanities Press International, Inc.,
1991.

Simon, Edith. *Luther Alive: Martin Luther and the Making of the Reformation.* Doubleday, 1968.

Stephens, W.P. *Zwingli: An Introduction to His Thought.* Oxford University Press, 1992.

Woolf, Bertram Lee. *Reformation Writings of Martin Luther.* Lutterworth Press, 1952.

FURTHER READING

PRIMARY SOURCES

Calvin, John. *Calvin's Commentaries*. Baker House, 1984.

———. *Institutes of the Christian Religion*, ed. Tony Lane and Hilary Osborne. Baker Book House, 1987.

Luther, Martin. *The Bondage of Will*. Fleming H. Revell Company, 1990.

———. *By Faith Alone*. Penguin USA, 1998.

———. *Christian Liberty*. Fortress Press, 1985.

———. *Luther's Large Catechism: A Contemporary Translation with Study Questions*. Concordia Publishing House, 1988.

———. *Luther's Prayers*. Fortress Press, 1994.

———. *Martin Luther, Selections from His Writings*, ed. John Dillenberger. Anchor, 1958.

SECONDARY SOURCES

Bainton, Roland. *Here I Stand: A Life of Martin Luther*. Abingdon Press, 1950.

Braaton, Carl E. *Principles of Lutheran Theology*. Fortress Press, 1983.

Carroll, James. *Constantine's Sword: The Church and the Jews: A History*. Houghton Mifflin, 2001.

Green, V.H.H. *Luther and the Reformation*. Capricorn Books, 1964.

Oberman, Heiko A. *Luther: Man Between God and the Devil*, trans. Eileen Walliser-Schwarzbart. Doubleday, 1992.

Ozment, Steven. *Protestants: The Birth of a Revolution*. Doubleday, 1992.

WEBSITES

A Mighty Fortress Is Our God: Martin Luther

http://www.luther.de/en/

Includes biographical information on Luther as well as legends, little-known facts, and texts of his writings and hymns.

Martin Luther: The Reluctant Revolutionary

http://www.pbs.org/empires/martinluther/

Includes detailed biographical information on Luther, as well as Luther-related activities and links to other Reformation resources.

Project Wittenberg

http://www.iclnet.org/pub/resources/text/wittenberg/wittenberg-home.html

An extensive collection of Luther's writings and Luther-related information.

Reformation

http://www.mun.ca/rels/hrollmann/reform/reform.html

Provides texts of many of Luther's writings, as well as links to sites about other Reformation figures, including John Calvin and Philip Melanchthon.

The Reformation in Germany

http://lcweb.loc.gov/exhibits/dres/dres3.html

Maintained by the Saxon State Library, includes information and links dealing with the Reformation and the lives of Luther and his contemporaries.

INDEX

INDEX

INDEX

INDEX

and Diet of Worms (1521), 42-
47, 57, 66
and Peace of Augsburg, 76-77,
78
and Peasants' Rebellion, 57-59,
61-63, 79-80
Nominalist movement, 20-21
nuns
and marriage to priests, 52, 54
and von Bora, 54-55, 57, 59-61

obedience
Luther on as German trait, 79-80
as monastic vow, 4, 9
Occam's razor, 20-21
Oelhafan, Sixtus, 45
omnipotent, Calvin on God as, 75
omniscient, Calvin on God as, 75
On the Jews and Their Lies, 70
Order of the Hermits of
St. Augustine, 10.
See also Augustinians
Otto I, 18, 41, 76
"Our God He Is a Castle Strong."
See "Mighty Fortress Is Our
God, A"

Palatinate, 46-47
Papal States, 15
Paul, St.
and letters to the Corinthians
and to the Galatians, 29, 49
and Luther, 16, 29, 30, 49, 51
Peace of Augsburg, 76-77, 78
peasants
and Peasants' Rebellion, 57-59,
61-63, 79-80
and potatoes, 78
Peasants' Rebellion/German
Peasants' War, 57-59, 61-63,
79-80

Pennsylvania, Lutheran congregation in, 75
Philadelphia, Lutheran congregation in, 75
Philip II, 77
Philip the Fair, 11
Pilgrims, 75
popes/papacy
in Avignon, 11
and bulls, 11, 14, 42
and conciliar movement, 11-12,
13-14, 21, 40, 45
Hus versus, 12, 13-14, 39, 42,
44
and Luther's German translation
of Bible, 54
Luther versus, 11-15, 39, 40, 42-
47, 54, 62, 106-114. *See also*
Catholic Church, and Luther;
Ninety-five Theses
and more than one pope, 11-12,
13-14
power of, 9, 11, 40
and Renaissance humanism,
14-15, 27, 39
and "Resolutions," 39
and Scriptures, 11, 40, 45
Wycliffe versus, 12-13.
See also Catholic Church
potatoes, peasants planting, 78
poverty, as monastic vow, 4,
9-10
preaching, and Dominicans, 10
predestination, Calvin on, 75
Presbyterian Church, 75
priests, and marriage to nuns, 52,
54
printing press, 38
Protestant Reformation. *See*
Calvinism; Lutheran Reformation
Puritans, 75

ABOUT THE CONTRIBUTORS

SAMUEL WILLARD CROMPTON teaches history at Holyoke Community College in western Massachusetts. He is the author or editor of many books, with titles that range from *100 Spiritual Leaders who Shaped World History* to *The Transforming Power of the Printing Press*. He attended the 1997 conference "Spirituality in Education," held at Naropa Institute in Boulder, Colorado.

MARTIN E. MARTY is an ordained minister in the Evangelical Lutheran Church and the Fairfax M. Cone Distinguished Service Professor Emeritus at the University of Chicago Divinity School, where he taught for thirty-five years. Marty has served as president of the American Academy of Religion, the American Society of Church History, and the American Catholic Historical Association, and was also a member of two U.S. presidential commissions. He is currently Senior Regent at St. Olaf College in Northfield, Minnesota. Marty has written more than fifty books, including the three-volume *Modern American Religion* (University of Chicago Press). His book *Righteous Empire* was a recipient of the National Book Award.